THE NEW ECONOMY BEYOND THE HYPE

The OECD Growth Project

OECD

ORGANISATION FOR ECONOMIC CO-OPERATION AND DEVELOPMENT

ORGANISATION FOR ECONOMIC CO-OPERATION AND DEVELOPMENT

Pursuant to Article 1 of the Convention signed in Paris on 14th December 1960, and which came into force on 30th September 1961, the Organisation for Economic Co-operation and Development (OECD) shall promote policies designed:

- to achieve the highest sustainable economic growth and employment and a rising standard of living in Member countries, while maintaining financial stability, and thus to contribute to the development of the world economy;

- to contribute to sound economic expansion in Member as well as non-member countries in the process of economic development; and

- to contribute to the expansion of world trade on a multilateral, non-discriminatory basis in accordance with international obligations.

The original Member countries of the OECD are Austria, Belgium, Canada, Denmark, France, Germany, Greece, Iceland, Ireland, Italy, Luxembourg, the Netherlands, Norway, Portugal, Spain, Sweden, Switzerland, Turkey, the United Kingdom and the United States. The following countries became Members subsequently through accession at the dates indicated hereafter: Japan (28th April 1964), Finland (28th January 1969), Australia (7th June 1971), New Zealand (29th May 1973), Mexico (18th May 1994), the Czech Republic (21st December 1995), Hungary (7th May 1996), Poland (22nd November 1996), Korea (12th December 1996) and the Slovak Republic (14th December 2000). The Commission of the European Communities takes part in the work of the OECD (Article 13 of the OECD Convention).

Publié en français sous le titre :
LA NOUVELLE ÉCONOMIE : MYTHE OU RÉALITÉ ?
Le rapport de l'OCDE sur la croissance

Foreword

At its meeting of May 1999, the Ministerial Council asked the OECD to analyse the causes underlying differences in growth performance in OECD countries and identify factors, institutions and policies that could enhance long-term growth prospects. In response to this request, the OECD launched a two-year study involving three Directorates and a number of Committees. A first report entitled Is There a New Economy? was presented to the Ministerial Council in June 2000. This Final Report, entitled The New Economy: Beyond the Hype draws the main policy conclusions from the two-year project.

The report draws on work carried out across the OECD, notably in the Economics Department, the Directorate for Science, Technology and Industry, and the Directorate for Education, Employment, Labour and Social Affairs. The principal authors of this report were Rory Clarke, Martine Durand, Dirk Pilat and Raymond Torres. Deborah Bloch and Susan Gascard provided excellent assistance. Contributions and comments were received from across the OECD Secretariat. Drafts of this report were discussed by the Economic Policy Committee, the Employment, Labour and Social Affairs Committee, the Committee for Industry and Business Environment, the Committee for Scientific and Technological Policy, and the Committee for Information, Computers and Communications Policy. Participants at these meetings provided useful comments.

Preface

At its meeting of May 1999, the Ministerial Council asked the OECD to analyse the causes underlying differences in growth performance in OECD countries and identify factors, institutions and policies that could enhance long-term growth prospects. In response to this request, the OECD launched a two-year study involving three Directorates and a number of Committees. A first report entitled "Is There a New Economy?" was presented to the Ministerial Council in June 2000.

This report draws the main policy conclusions from the two-year project. It complements the OECD report on Sustainable Development, which provides policy directions on how economic growth can be balanced with environmental goals. Well-designed and coherent policies in both areas would allow for economic development, environmental protection and social progress to be mutually supportive. Together, the two reports present a concrete policy agenda for the years to come.

Table of Contents

Introduction

The present slowdown in the United States has laid to rest one of the main myths of the last five years: the business cycle is not dead. But the slowdown should not distract from the fundamental question in this report of what structural shifts, if any, have taken place in growth patterns in OECD economies in recent years, and indeed, what implications those shifts hold for policymakers.

The question presupposes an understanding of the sources of growth, of what causes one developed economy to grow more rapidly than another. Why, for instance, did Ireland, which a decade ago was one of the OECD's poorer countries, see such a sharp rise in its GDP per head? Was it just a question of catch-up? If so, how did the United States, a country already in the lead in terms of GDP per capita, suddenly appear to find a new gear in the 1990s and forge further ahead of some major EU economies? That this extra growth delivered both low unemployment and low inflation makes the US case all the more intriguing. Some point to the role of new technology and innovation, but if that were the only answer, then why did growth languish in Japan, which has a large and successful computer hardware industry, but soar in Australia, which has virtually no such sector at all?

The causes of these diverging growth patterns are not easy to pinpoint. Some cite political and economic shocks as an explanation, like German unification or the Asian crisis. But these cannot explain why the US economy grew so fast in the last five years by comparison with its own historical standards or account for more rapid growth in a string of other OECD economies, particularly Australia, Ireland and the Netherlands. As this report shows, the key factor to examine is productivity, for if this shows an increase, then faster rates of non-inflationary economic expansion can be achieved. Most of the attention in recent years has focused on the sharp rise in investment in information and communications technology in several OECD countries and its possible effects on productivity. Before, as Nobel prize-winning economist, Robert Solow, famously put it in 1987, computers were everywhere except in the productivity statistics. By the end of the 1990s evidence of ICT-driven productivity growth began to emerge, leading some to argue that after years of investment in new technology, a higher growth path had been reached and a new economy had finally been born.

9

There is always a risk of exaggerating the potential of new technologies, and the boom in ICT investment over the past decade was accompanied by hype in some quarters. The slowdown in the United States has instilled realism in the debate, as well as putting an end to some exuberant economic behaviour. But it would be wrong to conclude that there was nothing particularly exceptional about the recent US experience, that the new economy was in fact a myth. Some of the arguments posited by new economy sceptics are of course true: the effect of ICT may be no greater than other important inventions of the past, like electricity generation and the internal combustion engine. Moreover, far greater productivity surges were recorded in previous decades, not least in the period before the 1970s.

Nevertheless, the evidence suggests that something new is taking place in the structure of OECD economies. Furthermore, it is this transformation that might account for the high growth recorded in several OECD countries. A surge in hardware and software investment is one consideration, while ICT appears to have brought "soft" economic benefits too, like valuable networks between suppliers and more choice for consumers, notably thanks to the Internet. Crucially, ICT seems to have facilitated productivity enhancing changes in the firm, in both new and traditional industries, but only when accompanied with greater skills and changes in the organisation of work. Consequently, policies that engage ICT, human capital, innovation and entrepreneurship in the growth process, alongside fundamental policies to control inflation and instil competition, while controlling public finances are likely to bear the most fruit over the longer term.

The key to remember is that acting in one of these areas alone is not enough to improve growth. Indeed, the policies advocated in this report are mutually reinforcing. The new growth opportunities can only be seized through a comprehensive strategy based on a policy mix that is suited to each country or circumstance.

Chapter I of the report examines the facts about growth in GDP per capita in OECD .countries over the past decade. The chapter shows that beyond established factors, such as labour utilisation and capital accumulation, investment in ICT and human capital, together with more efficient and innovative ways of producing goods and services, are essential to explaining the diverging patterns of OECD growth since the start of the 1990s.

Chapters II to V explore how ICT, human capital, innovation and business creation might be harnessed to achieve higher levels of economic growth. Chapter II examines the kinds of policies that are needed to enhance the wider diffusion of ICT. Chapter III argues that policies on innovation have a key role to play to ensure that new technologies and new knowledge continue to evolve and expand. Chapter IV looks at how human capital can promote growth. It stresses the role of education and training policies in meeting today's skill requirements and highlights how labour market institutions might respond to the changing nature of work. Chapter V focuses on the role of new and innovative firms in the growth process and identifies some of the policies and institutions that are conducive to business creation and dynamic economic activity.

Chapter VI warns that getting the economic and social fundamentals right is vital for growth to take place. Today's new economic environment depends as much as ever on sound macroeconomic management, well-functioning markets and openness to international trade, competition and, of course, change. It pinpoints the role of government, as one of the key players in the growth process, and in ensuring that the benefits of growth are widely shared. A short set of conclusions completes the study.

Chapter I.

Growth Patterns in the OECD Area

In examining growth patterns today, it is helpful to remember that economic growth in the OECD area has varied considerably over time. In the 1950s and 1960s, most OECD countries grew rapidly as they recovered from the war and applied US technology and knowledge to upgrade their economies. Growth of GDP per capita – the key yardstick of economic performance – in Western Europe reached almost 4 per cent annually over the 1950-73 period, and OECD countries in Southern Europe, as well as Japan and Korea grew even more rapidly (Maddison, 1995). This catch-up period came to a halt in the 1970s; in fact, average growth rates of GDP per capita over the 1973-92 period for much of the OECD area were only half that of the preceding period.

In the past decade, a few OECD countries, including the United States, have seen an acceleration in growth of GDP per capita. On the other hand, some of the other major economies have lagged. This divergence has caused renewed interest in the main factors driving economic growth and the policies that might influence it. This report shows that these growth patterns are a reflection of structural shifts in the factors and policies that drive economic growth; understanding them better provides valuable lessons for policymaking, even if some OECD economies may be slowing down.

I.1. Growth in the OECD area has been uneven

In 1999, the United States had the highest level of GDP per capita in the OECD area (Figure I.1). There is nothing new about this: the United States has had the highest level of GDP per capita in the OECD area for the past five decades. However, the gap between the US level and that of other major OECD countries has widened markedly since the early 1990s, as underlying growth in some economies, particularly Japan and Germany, slowed in the 1990s when compared with the 1980s. The wide differences in income levels in 1999 therefore partly reflect large discrepancies in growth patterns in the OECD area over the past decade.

Figure I.1. **Large differentials in GDP per capita**

Levels of PPP-based GDP per capita with respect to the United States, 1999

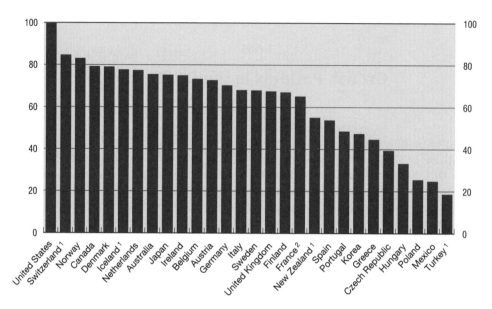

Note: *The United States had the highest level of GDP per capita in 1999, followed by Switzerland and Norway.*
Most OECD countries, including all other G7 countries, have income levels that range between 65 and
80 per cent of the United States
1. GDP is based on the 1968 System of National Accounts (SNA). The level of GDP per capita of these countries is
likely to be somewhat underestimated.
2. Includes overseas departments.
Source: OECD, *National Accounts of OECD Countries, Main Aggregates, Volume 1.*

This becomes clearer when comparing *trend* growth, *i.e.* growth rates adjusted for the business cycle. Three OECD countries – Australia, Ireland and the Netherlands – registered markedly stronger growth of GDP per capita over the past decade compared with the 1980s (Figure I.2). Several other countries also experienced some improvement. This includes the United States, where trend growth accelerated strongly in the second half of the decade. In contrast, the increase in GDP per capita in many other OECD countries, including Japan and much of Europe, slowed, in some cases quite markedly so. In several countries, such as Finland, Canada, Greece, Iceland and Sweden, a pick-up in trend growth of GDP per capita became only apparent in the second half of the 1990s.

Figure I.2. **Uneven trend growth of GDP per capita**
Total economy, percentage change at annual rate

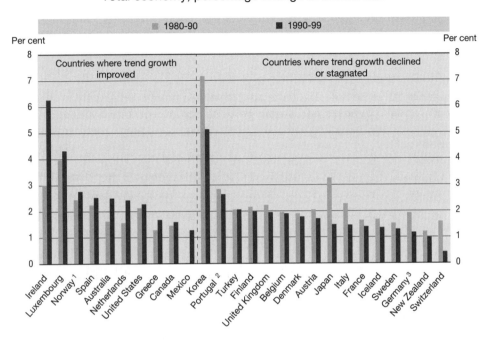

Note: Trend growth in the 1990s was higher than in the 1980s in several countries: Australia, Canada, Greece,
Ireland, Luxembourg, Mexico, the Netherlands, Norway, Spain and the United States. But trend growth
declined substantially in Italy, Switzerland, Japan and Korea. The decline in trend growth in Germany is
influenced by the unification process.
1. Total Norway.
2. 1990-98.
3. West Germany for 1980-90; Germany for 1991-99.
Source: OECD, based on data for the OECD Economic Outlook, No. 68. See Scarpetta et al. (2000) for details.

The acceleration in trend growth in the United States over the 1990s has attracted
a lot of attention. And with good reason, as the United States already had the world's
highest level of GDP per capita in 1990, and so had no catching up to do. Indeed the
country has been pushing the technological frontier in many fields. The rise in trend
growth in the 1990s was the longest upswing in US modern history, and while it may
now have come to an end, claims that a new economy has emerged in the United States
have had to be looked at seriously. Moreover, why have some OECD countries
experienced more rapid growth of GDP per capita in the 1990s, while other countries
have slowed down?

I.2. What explains the differences?

The growth divergence is not simply a reflection of different measurement techniques used in different OECD countries, as Box I.1 shows. Rather, part of the OECD area's diverging growth patterns of the 1990s can be explained by the differences in labour productivity growth and labour utilisation (Figure I.3). The United States, together with a few other countries, improved its labour productivity and labour utilisation at the same time – *i.e.* more people worked more productively. In contrast, some European countries had strong productivity growth, but low employment growth, particularly in the first half of the 1990s. Their higher productivity growth may have been achieved by a greater use of capital or by dismissing (or not employing) low-productivity workers. In short, countries with higher growth rates of GDP per capita typically maintained or increased labour utilisation over the 1990s.

Box I.1. **Do diverging growth rates simply reflect different measurement techniques?**

Some studies have suggested that the strong growth record of the United States reflects the way its GDP is measured. This is unlikely. Almost all OECD countries have now adopted the 1993 System of National Accounts, which implies that the framework for the measurement of GDP levels is broadly the same across countries. Nevertheless, two important caveats might affect comparisons of GDP growth.

First, the measurement of prices does indeed differ across countries. Prices are fundamental in calculating GDP growth, as they help to separate real changes from nominal ones. Where OECD countries differ is in how they measure price changes for rapidly evolving goods and services, such as computers. France and the United States, for instance, use specially designed "hedonic" deflators for such goods: these deflators adjust their price changes for key characteristics, like processing speed and disk capacity. They tend to show faster declines in computer prices than conventional price indexes, and that means higher real growth. As a result, countries that use hedonic indexes are likely to record faster real growth in investment and production of information and communications technology (ICT) than countries that do not use them (Schreyer, 2000*a*). However, while hedonic price indexes may have a large impact on ICT investment, they have only a small impact on estimates of total GDP, usually of the order of 0.1 to 0.2 percentage points (Schreyer, 2001). Overall cross-country comparisons of GDP should still be valid as a result.

A second caveat is that the base period for the calculation of growth rates differs across countries. Several OECD countries use fixed-weight indexes, where prices and quantities of a particular year are compared with the first or last year of the period

---

Box I.1.   **Do diverging growth rates simply reflect different measurement techniques?** (*cont.*)

under review. Other countries use chain-linked indexes, where only adjacent years are directly compared and non-adjacent years are compared by linking the indexes for adjacent years. There is little difference between these two methods as long as relative prices between goods remain stable. However, when there is a change in relative prices of the goods that make up the basket, fixed-weighted volume indices tend to place too much weight on goods or services for which relative prices have fallen. In other words, they would exaggerate the effect on GDP growth of a long-term fall in ICT prices, for instance. Chain-weighted volume indices, on the other hand, successively reduce the weight of items whose relative prices fall. This can have large impacts on measured GDP growth. For example, the official chain-weighted index for the United States shows a growth rate for GDP of 4.3 per cent for 1997-98, but a fixed-weighted index based on 1990 prices shows a growth rate of 6.5 per cent for the same year (Whelan, 2000).

There is little or no reason to argue that the United States overestimates its GDP growth compared with other OECD countries, since it uses chain-weighted indexes in combination with its hedonic price index for computers. The effect of these two methods on GDP growth should be minor as they broadly balance each other out (Schreyer, 2001). This shows that the variation in growth of GDP per capita between OECD countries cannot be explained away by measurement differences.

As well as growth differences, labour utilisation and labour productivity can also help to explain the large gap in income levels in 1999. Take France, Italy, Belgium and the Netherlands for instance. Despite having high productivity levels, their lower employment rates and shorter working hours help explain the bulk of the income gap with the United States, whose labour utilisation rate was higher (Scarpetta, *et al.*, 2000). As for the laggard countries at the lower end of Figure I.1, their low levels of labour productivity are the main reason for the large gap in income levels. On the positive side, the large gaps suggest there is scope for further growth in virtually all OECD countries.

How to achieve higher growth and reduce these gaps is the challenge. The role of labour utilisation was already discussed above. Labour productivity, meanwhile, can be lifted in several ways: by improving the quality of labour used in the production process, increasing the use of capital and improving its quality, and attaining greater overall efficiency in how these factors of production are used together, what economists call multi-factor productivity (MFP).[1] MFP reflects many types of efficiency

17

Figure I.3.   **Changes in labour utilisation contribute to trend growth in GDP per capita**

Total economy, percentage change at annual rates, 1990-99 [1]

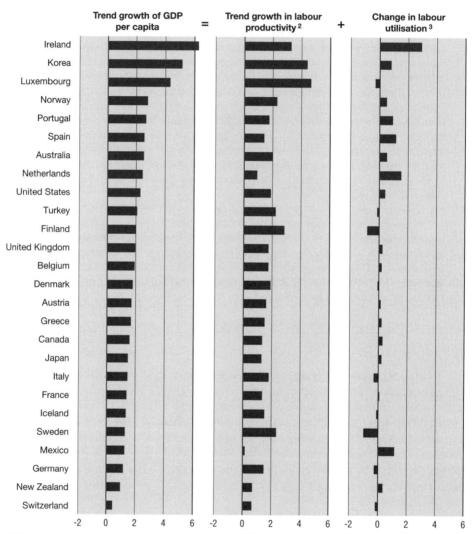

Note: The graph shows the breakdown of trend growth in GDP per capita in the trends in labour utilisation and GDP per person employed. High growth in Ireland, Mexico, the Netherlands and Spain was supported by increased labour utilisation. Finland, Italy and Sweden suffered from a decline in labour utilisation over the 1990s.

1. 1991-99 for Germany; 1990-98 for Korea and Portugal.
2. Trend growth in GDP per person employed.
3. Trend growth in labour utilisation, measured as persons employed to the total population.

Source: OECD, based on data for the OECD *Economic Outlook,* No. 68.

improvements, such as improved managerial practices, organisational changes and innovative ways of producing goods and services.

The quality of labour, usually referred to as human capital, is the first factor that plays a fundamental role in labour productivity growth. The rise in the educational attainment among workers over the 1990s is only one sign of this role (Figure I.4); increases in the level of post-educational skills may be even more important, although few hard measures are available. Another reason is technology: the demand for more and better skills has risen in response to more and better technology. Improvements in the quality of labour have directly contributed to growth in virtually all OECD countries (Scarpetta *et al.*, 2000).

Investment in physical capital is the second factor that plays an important role. It expands and renews the existing capital stock and enables new technologies to

Figure I.4. **The level of education of the population has increased**

Average number of years of education of the working-age population

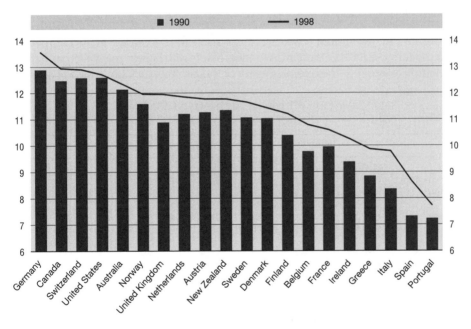

Note: The graph shows that the average number of years of education of the working-age population has increased considerably over the 1990s.

Source: OECD, see Bassanini and Scarpetta (2001).

enter the production process. While some countries have experienced an overall increase in the contribution of capital to growth over the past decade, ICT has typically been the most dynamic area of investment. This reflects rapid technological progress and strong competitive pressure in the production of ICT goods and services and a consequent steep decline in prices. This fall, together with the growing scope for application of ICT, has encouraged investment in ICT, at times shifting investment away from other assets. The available data for OECD countries show that ICT investment rose from less than 15 per cent of total non-residential investment in the business sector in the early 1980s, to between 15 and 35 per cent in 1999 (Colecchia, 2001).

While ICT investment accelerated in most OECD countries, the pace of that investment and its impact on growth differed widely (Table I.1). For the countries for which data are available, ICT investment accounted for between 0.3 and 0.9 percentage point of growth in GDP per capita over the 1995-99 period. The United States, Australia and Finland received the largest boost; Japan, Germany, France and Italy the smallest. Estimates for the United Kingdom (Oulton, 2001) suggest that the role of ICT investment was larger in that country over 1994-98 than in other major EU countries. A study for the Netherlands suggests only a small role for ICT investment over 1996-99 (Van der Wiel, 2000). Software accounted for up to a third of the overall contribution of ICT investment to GDP growth in OECD countries.

The shift in investment towards ICT has also led to a change in the composition of the capital stock in OECD countries towards assets with higher "marginal" productivity, i.e. an improvement in the overall quality of the capital stock (Scarpetta et al., 2000).

Table I.1. **ICT capital has boosted GDP growth**
Percentage points contribution to annual average GDP growth, business sector

		United States	Japan	Germany	France	Italy	Canada	Australia	Finland
IT and communications equipment	1990-95	0.3	0.2	0.2	0.2	0.2	0.3	0.3	0.2
	1995-99	0.6	0.3	0.2	0.2	0.2	0.4	0.4	0.4
Software	1990-95	0.1	0.1	0.1	0.0	0.0	n.a.	0.1	0.1
	1995-99	0.3	0.0	0.1	0.1	0.1	n.a.	0.2	0.2
Total ICT	1990-95	0.4	0.3	0.3	0.2	0.2	n.a.	0.5	0.2
	1995-99	0.9	0.3	0.3	0.4	0.3	n.a.	0.6	0.6

Note: The table compares the contribution of ICT capital to GDP growth for eight countries, differentiating between the role of ICT hardware and software. It shows that ICT contributed 0.9 percentage point to US GDP growth, three times more than in Japan, Germany and Italy. Australia and Finland also received large contributions of ICT investment in GDP growth. The estimates are based on a harmonised deflator for ICT investment, adjusting for cross-country differences in methods (see Box 1.1). Methodological differences in measuring software investment may affect the results, however. The estimates are not adjusted for the business cycle and therefore not directly comparable with the graphs in this Chapter.

Source: Colecchia (2001).

The improvement in quality implies that investment in ICT has had larger effects on GDP growth than similar investment in other assets would have had. In the United States, over the 1995-99 period, increased quality is estimated to account for over 0.5 percentage point of the total contribution of capital to GDP growth, of 1.7 percentage points. In Australia, about one-quarter of the 1.6 percentage points contribution of capital to GDP growth over 1990-99 is estimated to be due to improved quality.

The final factor that accounts for some of the pick-up in labour productivity growth is a faster increase in trend multi-factor productivity growth in the 1990s. MFP growth rose particularly in Australia, Canada, Denmark, Finland, Ireland and Sweden, but also in Norway, the United States and New Zealand (Figure I.5). In the second half of the 1990s, the trend in MFP improved further in several countries. There are many reasons for this. Better skills and better technology may have caused the blend

Figure I.5.   **Trend multi-factor productivity growth increased in many countries**

Average annual percentage change from 1980-90 to 1990-99

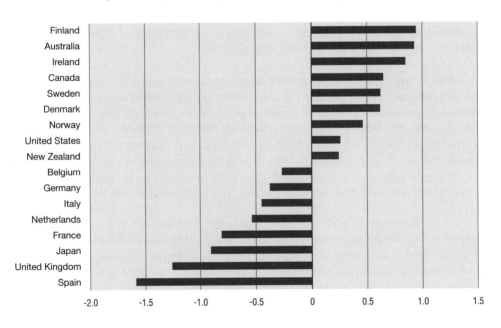

Note: The graph shows that MFP growth increased markedly between the 1980s and 1990s in Finland, Australia and Ireland. It decreased sharply in Spain, the United Kingdom and Japan. In the Netherlands and Spain, MFP growth declined but growth of GDP per capita improved due to increased use of labour and capital. The estimates are adjusted for hours worked and are based on trend series.

Source: OECD, based on data for the OECD Economic Outlook, No. 68, see Scarpetta et al. (2000) for details.

21

of labour and capital to produce more efficiently, organisational and managerial changes may have helped to improve operations, and innovation may have led to more valuable output being produced with a given combination of capital and labour. Most of these factors will be discussed later in this report. But as MFP growth is measured as a residual, in that it is the number that is left after the contributions of increased labour and capital have been accounted for, it is difficult to provide hard evidence on all of these factors. Some is available, though.

First, in some OECD countries, MFP reflects rapid technological progress in the production of ICT. Technological progress at Intel, for instance, has enabled the amount of transistors packed on a microprocessor to double every 18 months since 1965, and even more rapidly so since 1995. While the ICT sector is relatively small in most OECD countries (OECD, 2000a), it can make a large contribution to growth if it expands much more rapidly than other sectors. In the United States, for instance, MFP growth in the ICT-producing sector explains about 0.2-0.3 percentage point of the overall pick-up in MFP growth since 1995 (US Council of Economic Advisors, 2001). Some other OECD countries, such as Finland, have also benefited from rapid MFP growth in the ICT-producing sector (Pilat and Lee, 2001; OECD, 2000b). The impact of innovation on MFP is not limited to the ICT sector but is felt throughout the economy. Moreover, investment in innovation both at home and abroad also drives MFP growth (Guellec and Van Pottelsberghe, 2001).

MFP also reflects competition. Analysis of productivity growth shows that the effects of competition, such as the entry and exit of firms and changes in market shares are important drivers of productivity growth (OECD, 2001a). New firms typically use a more efficient mix of labour, capital and technology than existing firms, which in the long term has a positive effect on MFP growth. This is particularly true of emerging industries, such as ICT-related ones, where new firms play an important role in productivity growth. In contrast, growth in mature industries is typically driven by productivity growth within existing firms or by the exit of obsolete firms.

The third driver of MFP that can be identified, albeit with less accuracy, is the use of ICT in the production process. If the rise in MFP due to ICT were little more than a reflection of rapid technological progress in the production of computers, semi-conductors and related products and services, there would be no effects of ICT use on MFP in countries that are not already producers of ICT. For ICT to have benefits on MFP in countries that do not produce ICT goods, it needs to have spill-over – or network – effects linked to its use in the production process. These spill-over effects have proven difficult to identify over the past decade, even though ICT has diffused rapidly (Box I.2). In recent years some evidence from firm-level and sectoral studies has emerged that the growth in MFP may also be linked to the productivity-enhancing benefits from the use and diffusion of ICT (OECD, 2000c; Figure I.6).

Figure I.6.   **Pick-up in MFP growth and increase in ICT use**

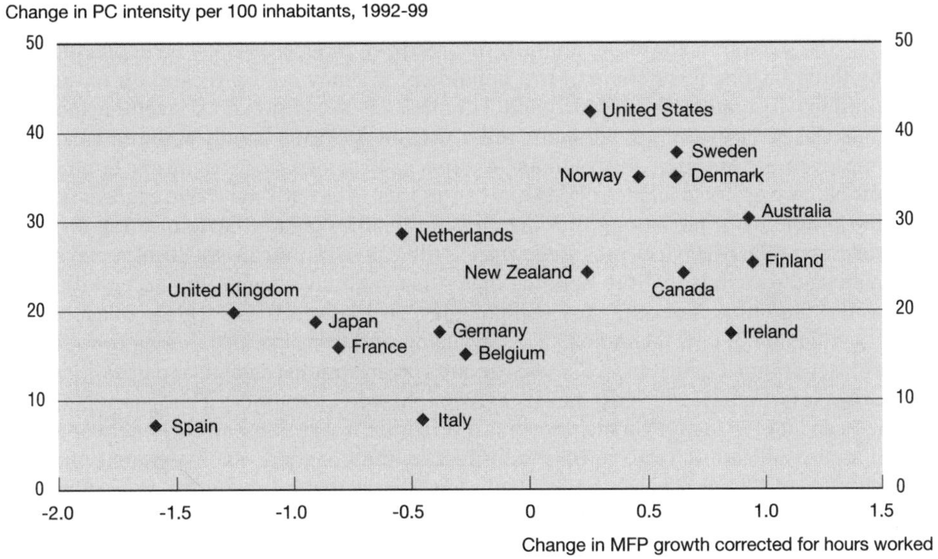

Change in PC intensity per 100 inhabitants, 1992-99

Note: Countries with the largest increase in the penetration of PCs in the 1990s have experienced a more rapid pick-up in MFP growth between the 1980s and the 1990s. Correlation coefficient: 0.61; T statistic: 3.0.

Source: Figure I.5 and OECD Information Technology Outlook 2000.

Box I.2.   **The Solow Paradox: does it still apply?**

The Solow paradox, attributed to economist Robert Solow who once observed that computers are everywhere except in the productivity data, was appropriate during much of the 1980s and early 1990s, when the rapid diffusion of computing technology seemed to have little impact on MFP growth. Does the recent surge in MFP growth in some OECD countries imply that this paradox has been resolved? Only partially. Although MFP has improved, it has done so in only a small number of OECD countries. In some countries, high MFP growth in ICT production explains some of the surge in overall MFP growth. In addition, certain ICT-using services, such as wholesale and retail trade, have experienced an above-average pick-up in MFP growth in recent years, e.g. in the United States, Australia and Finland. There is also evidence at the firm level and from case studies that ICT can help to improve the overall efficiency of capital and labour. But it remains unclear how much of the pick-up in MFP growth can be accounted for by ICT as opposed to other factors, such as increased R&D or improved organisation.

Box I.2.   **The Solow Paradox: does it still apply?** (*cont.*)

The paradox is therefore not fully resolved yet, though this may be explained by three factors. First, some of the benefits of ICT may not be picked up in the productivity statistics (Triplett, 1999). For instance, the improved convenience of financial services due to automatic teller machines (ATMs) is only counted as an improvement in the quality of financial services in some OECD countries. Similar problems exist for insurance and business services. In fact, ICT may have aggravated the problems of measuring productivity, as it allows greater customisation and differentiation of services provided, which is difficult to capture in statistical surveys. A second reason is that the benefits of ICT use might take some time to emerge, as did the impacts of other key technologies, such as electricity. This is because the diffusion of new technologies is often slow and firms can take a long time to adjust to them. For instance, ICT use requires organisational change and upskilling of workers, none of which can be done overnight (see Chapter IV). Third, assuming ICT can lift MFP in part via the networks it provides, it takes time to build networks that are sufficiently large to have an effect on the economy. As investment and diffusion of ICT was high in the 1990s, networks have probably broadened, suggesting that computers may show up much more clearly in the productivity statistics in the near future.

I.3. Summing up

This section has shown that the causes of more rapid growth are several. In particular, those OECD countries that registered increased growth in GDP per capita in the 1990s did so by having generally drawn more people into employment, accumulating more capital, in particular ICT, and improving the average quality of their work force. In many cases, they have also improved MFP. Some of these factors are well established as drivers of growth; others have received a new emphasis in recent years. In several countries with strong growth in the 1990s, ICT investment has been important. This has led to a rapid diffusion of ICT, which has also affected overall efficiency. Innovation and technology diffusion are also important, as a possible way to higher MFP and to future technological breakthroughs. Education and skills have also gained new significance, partly due to the diffusion of new technologies. In addition, MFP growth in new industries has been accompanied by the creation of start-up firms. But to have any chance of succeeding in ICT, innovation, human capital and firm creation, governments must ensure that the fundamentals – macroeconomic stability, openness and competition, as well as economic and social institutions – are working properly. Many of the countries that improved growth performance in the 1990s did so because they had been able to get the fundamentals right; they had created an environment that could take advantage of the new technologies and business opportunities when they emerged. Moreover, strong fundamentals allowed these countries to improve productivity while simultaneously drawing more people into productive employment.

Note

1. Multi-factor productivity is also referred to as total factor productivity. MFP differs from labour productivity in that it reflects the combined efficiency of both labour *and* capital. It is a better yardstick than labour productivity, as labour productivity growth can also be achieved by employing more capital or by dismissing workers with below-average productivity. MFP is more difficult to measure, however, and labour productivity growth is often used as a proxy for MFP growth.

Chapter II.

Seizing the Benefits of ICT

II.1. ICT has contributed to growth

ICT is transforming economic activity, as the steam engine, railways and electricity have done in the past. ICT has already had important economic impacts. It has contributed significantly to high growth in several OECD countries in the past few years. It has been a catalyst of change in business, improving work organisation for instance, helping firms to reduce routine transaction costs and rationalise their supply chains. It has spurred innovation in services and made manufacturing and design more efficient. Inventories and overheads have become more manageable. Moreover, ICT has spawned value-generating networks between producers and consumers. Such benefits are long-term in their effects, and will continue to develop, even if investment in ICT tapers off in some countries.

It is too early to say how important ICT is compared with previous new technologies. What is important is that ICT appears to be an important transformational technology today. As this report explains, governments have to ensure they have the policies in place to seize the benefits of ICT, as well as limit any negative effects. As with any technology that is based on networks – and the Internet is that *par excellence* – the more people that use it, the more benefits it generates. Encouraging the use of ICT, by increasing competition to bring down costs and by building confidence, should therefore be an important policy aim. It is also important to recall that the development of ICT partly resulted from policy efforts in some OECD countries to create a more innovative economy. Governments should help to build an environment that is both conducive to innovation and adaptable to future technological breakthroughs; such policies are discussed in the next Chapter.

II.2. Competition encourages ICT investment and use

Despite the emerging benefits of ICT, some OECD countries have been slow to embrace it. There are several reasons for this, a lack of ICT skills, limited capacity to adjust the production process to ICT technologies, or poor access to finance, being just three typical ones that will be discussed in this report. Insufficient competition may be another factor, because this can harm efficiency and slow the adoption of new techniques. Indeed, the United States may have benefited first from ICT investment ahead of other OECD countries, as it already had a high level of competition in the 1980s, which it strengthened through regulatory reforms in the 1980s and 1990s. Globalisation, although common to all OECD countries, has added to this process, by forcing firms to look more and more to innovation and technology to help them restructure and thrive.

Firms in the United States and Canada have enjoyed considerably lower costs of ICT investment goods in the 1990s than firms in European countries and Japan (Figure II.1). These low costs may have helped to stimulate investment in both countries. Barriers to trade, in particular non-tariff barriers related to standards, import licensing and

Figure II.1. **The price of ICT investment**

Price differentials with the United States, average of estimates for 1993 and 1996

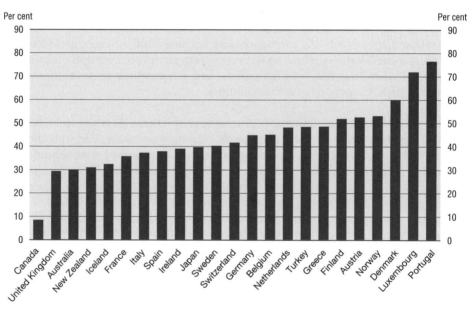

Note: Relative price differences in office and data processing machinery (here, on the basis of detailed purchasing power parities for 1993 and 1996) in the mid-1990s may help explain some of the discrepancy in ICT diffusion between OECD countries. US prices were the lowest by far, while prices in Japan and Germany were some 40 per cent higher than in the United States. But prices were higher still in Finland, which is nonetheless sometimes considered as a "new economy" country. Differences in value-added taxation play some role, but other factors, such as competition, also come into play.

Source: OECD (1995; 2000d).

government procurement, may partly explain the cost differentials. The higher price levels in other OECD countries may also be associated with a lack of competition within countries.[1] In time, however, international trade and competition should erode these cross-country price differences; the evidence suggests that the prices of ICT investment goods in 1996 were already much closer to those in the United States than they were in 1993.[2] Since then, they have come down further across the OECD (Colecchia, 2001). Policy could help to accelerate this trend, by implementing a more active competition policy and measures to promote market openness, both domestically and internationally.

The investment and diffusion of ICT do not just depend on the cost of the investment goods themselves, but also on the associated costs of communication and use once the hardware is linked to a network. Increased competition in the telecommunications industry, thanks to extensive regulatory reform, has been of particular importance in driving down these costs. It has led to more entrants, greater technology diffusion, improved quality and a higher rate of innovation. This has benefited the industry, as well as the economy as a whole. Countries that moved early to liberalise their telecommunications industry now have much lower communications costs and, consequently, a wider usage and diffusion of ICT technologies than those that followed later on.

By the beginning of 2001, only three OECD countries (Turkey, Hungary and the Slovak Republic) still had monopolies in the provision of fixed network services. In the wireless sector, the last monopoly was already eliminated in 1998 (Figure II.2). This does not imply that effective competition will immediately take hold. In some countries, such as Finland, Germany, Japan, the United Kingdom and the United States, new entrants had already taken more than 30 per cent of the long-distance market in 1999. But in other countries, like Australia, Italy, Korea and Spain, the incumbent firm still held on to more than 80 per cent of the market in 1999, which could point to a lack of effective competition. Clearly, there is more to be done before competition in telecommunications markets takes hold in many OECD countries.

An example concerns the costs of leased lines. These lines are used to transport large volumes of information between firms and provide the building blocks for B2B electronic commerce (Box II.1). Liberalisation has significantly lowered the prices of leased lines in recent years, particularly following major communications reform in Europe since 1998. But prices continue to differ substantially between OECD countries (Figure II.3), and more will need to be done.

Another example concerns the costs of Internet access for consumers. These also differ considerably from country to country, reflecting fixed and variable telephone charges as set by telecommunications firms, but also the fees charged by the leading Internet service providers in each country – companies like AOL, World Online and

Figure II.2. Competition in OECD telecommunications markets is increasing

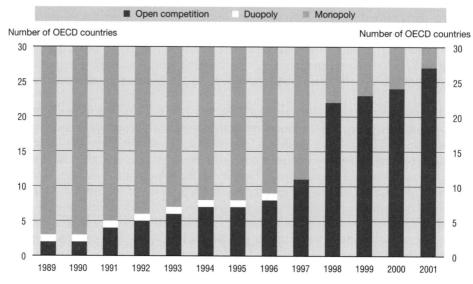

A. COMPETITION IN FIXED NETWORK INFRASTRUCTURE

■ Open competition □ Duopoly ▨ Monopoly

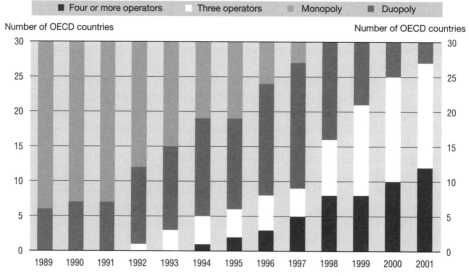

B. COMPETITION IN CELLULAR MOBILE INFRASTRUCTURE

■ Four or more operators □ Three operators ▨ Monopoly ▪ Duopoly

Note: There are no monopolies left in the wireless telecommunications sector, and the share of the market with four or more operators is rising. In the fixed-line area, open competition has spread fast, with only three monopolies left in 2001.

Source: OECD Communications Outlook 2001.

Box II.1.   **How important is e-commerce?**

While electronic commerce has grown rapidly, it is still quite small; indeed, too small to explain the pick-up in productivity growth discussed above. In the United States, for example, business-to-business (B2B) manufacturing shipments ordered online accounted for about 12 per cent of all manufacturing shipments in 1999. Business-to-consumer (B2C) is considerably smaller. In the United States, it accounted for about USD 25.9 billion over 2000, or about 0.8 per cent of total retail sales. In Denmark, electronic commerce accounted for about 1 per cent of business sales in 2000. It is smaller in other OECD countries. In Australia, around 0.4 per cent of all orders were received via the Internet in 1999-2000. And in Canada, around 0.4 per cent of all customer orders were received over the Internet in 2000.

Still, e-commerce has great growth potential in the longer term. The B2B part is particularly important. Preliminary results from a cross-country OECD project, based on a common methodology, show that it reduces the costs of transactions linked to the production and distribution of goods and services, and enables firms to manage their supply chains more effectively and communicate more easily (OECD, 2001*b*). An example is the optical networking industry in Canada, where inventories declined from 30-40 days a few years ago, to 9-12 days today. E-commerce may even spur competition, drive down prices and create larger, more transparent markets, with more choice and variety.

E-commerce is not just about new companies and innovative lines of business. Indeed, it is mainly about increasing efficiency in traditional sectors, *i.e.* the "old economy". One example is the automobile sector, where ICT has improved product development, procurement and supply. Car producers are now able to reduce the costs of intermediation, by limiting the number of dealers and salesmen. Cars will soon be sold online, with customers specifying the features they want from the options available and manufacturers building the car according to these specifications. The savings could be substantial. Korean car producers expect that the cost of procurement of maintenance, repair and operating supplies will decrease by 20 per cent following the adoption of e-commerce.

E-commerce also offers great potential for savings in services, such as the information-intensive health care sector. Estimates in the United States suggest that Internet-based processing of health claim forms could reduce the cost from USD 10-15 for paper claims down to USD 2-4 for claims processed to Electronic Data Interchange (EDI), and to just USD 2-4 cents for claims processed through the Internet (Litan and Rivlin, 2000).

Figure II.3. **The cost of leased lines in the OECD, August 2000**

Charges for a basket of national leased lines of 2 Megabits per second,
OECD average = 100

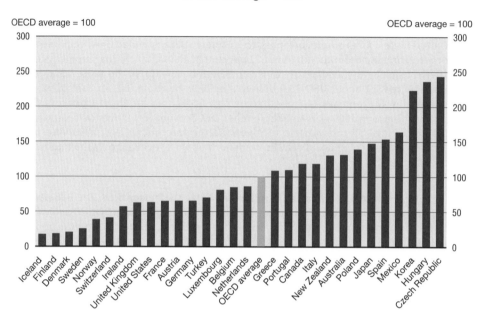

Note: *The graph shows the total charges (excluding taxes) within each country for a basket of national leased
lines that can carry two megabits of information per second. It shows that the Nordic countries have the
lowest charges for such lines. Hungary and the Czech Republic have the highest charges.*
Source: *OECD Communications Outlook 2001.*

Wanadoo (Figure II.4). Such cost differences also seem to affect the take-up of the
Internet; countries with lower access costs typically have more Internet hosts (Figure II.5).

National and international telecommunications markets are clearly opening up. The
next step is to introduce competition at local level. In 1999, new entrants had only a very
small share of local markets in virtually all OECD countries; only in Canada and the
United Kingdom did new entrants have more than 15 per cent of local markets (OECD,
2001c). More competition in the local loop would surely drive prices down further and
would help to change the pricing structure of the Internet. Take unmetered access to the
Internet (*i.e.* rather than pay charges by the minute, users pay either a flat fee or no fee
for unlimited Internet access). Australia, Canada, Mexico, New Zealand and the United States
have had such systems in place for some time. That means more time spent online. This
is good for B2C electronic commerce, whose development depends on users becoming
accustomed to the Internet, and feeling secure enough to take the time "to-shop-around".
Countries with unmetered access typically have more secure servers – which are needed

Figure II.4. **Access costs for the Internet in OECD countries differ considerably**

Costs for 40 hours of Internet use at peak times, September 2000, in USD PPP

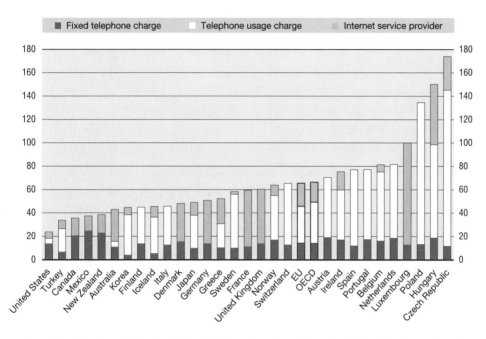

Note: Internet access costs differ substantially between OECD countries, primarily due to differences in variable
          telephone charges and the costs of Internet service providers. Previous OECD studies show that these
          differences are primarily due to the state of competition in different member countries.
Source: OECD Communications Outlook 2001.

for secure transactions on-line – and more rapid growth in secure servers (Figure II.6). Unmetered access options were available in 12 OECD countries by the beginning of 2001, up from the aforementioned five at the beginning of 2000 (OECD, 2001c).

The introduction of competition in local markets typically involves "unbundling", i.e. the separation of the local network and infrastructure from the services that are provided over that network. In other words, the operator of the local network should not have to be the same as the phone service provider. Unbundling enables new entrants to offer such services as unmetered Internet access to their customers should they so wish. Most OECD countries are now implementing unbundling, and the European Commission has mandated unbundling of the local loop for its member states as of the beginning of 2001. But this will not be simple; it will require further regulatory reform and better enforcement of competition law to promote vigorous competition and to create the conditions for future investment.[3]

_33_

Figure II.5.   **Countries with low access costs have a greater diffusion of the Internet**

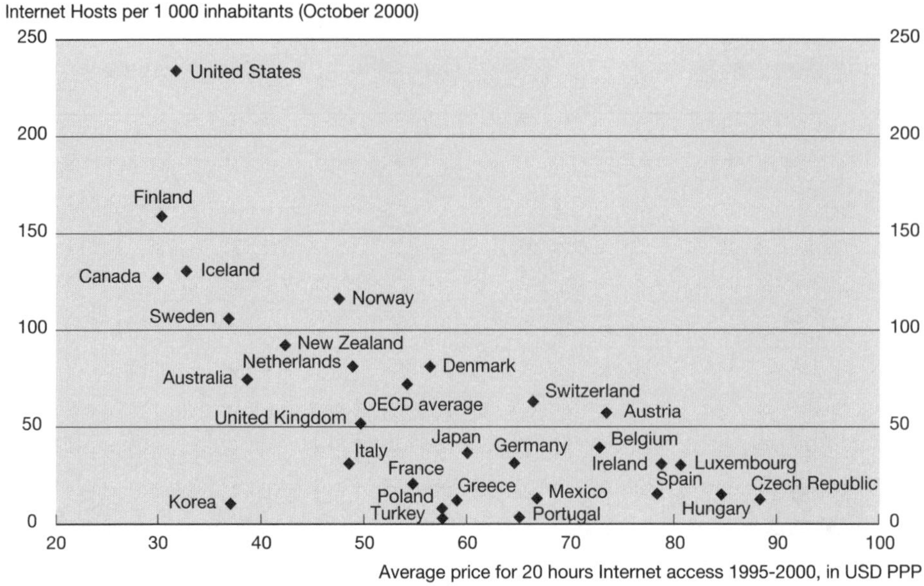

Internet Hosts per 1 000 inhabitants (October 2000)

Average price for 20 hours Internet access 1995-2000, in USD PPP

Note: *Countries with low average access costs over the 1995-2000 period, such as Canada, Finland and the United States, typically have more Internet hosts – a computer system connected to the Internet – than countries with high average costs. Other factors matter though; Korea now has low average access costs but still a low penetration of the Internet. Access costs include VAT, and cover both peak and off-peak.*
Source: OECD *(www.oecd.org/dsti/sti/it/cm)* and Telcordia Technologies *(www.netsizer.com).*

Another important policy challenge is to promote greater competition between different networks, *e.g.* fixed networks, cable television networks, satellites and wireless networks, so that users can choose. Both unbundling and competition between different networks will help in stimulating the development of high-speed access options, *e.g.* broadband technologies that enable access to multi-media applications, such as fibre optics. The competitive development and diffusion of these technologies would also help to spur e-commerce.

II.3. Building confidence in the use of ICT

Policies to increase competition will not on their own boost the diffusion of ICT or the use of e-commerce. An appropriate regulatory and legal environment is required too, particularly in the areas of privacy, security and consumer protection. The key word here is confidence, among consumers, business providers, and

Figure II.6.   **Electronic commerce has developed rapidly in some countries**

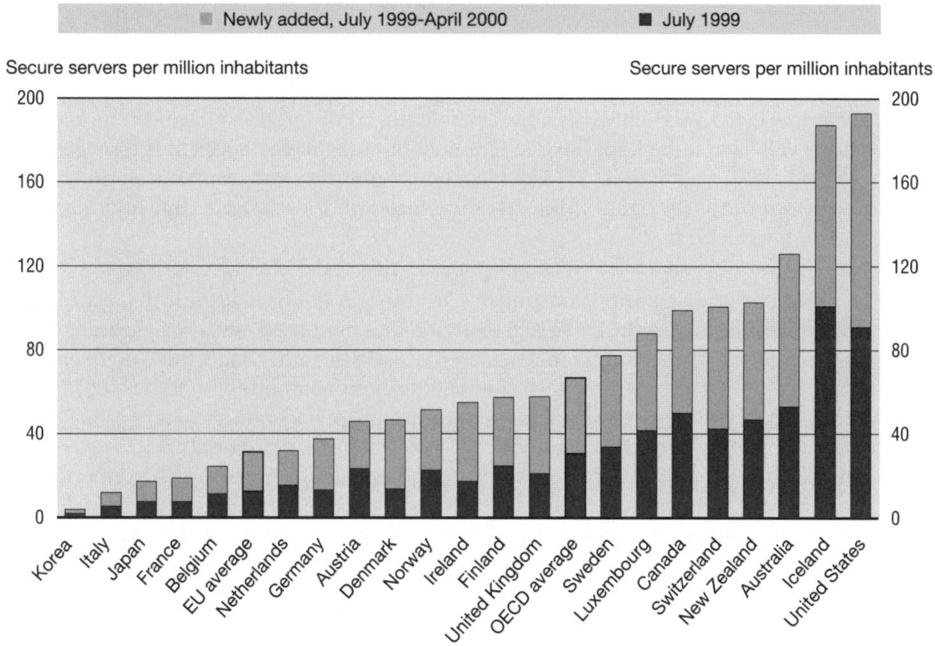

| Newly added, July 1999-April 2000 | July 1999 |

Secure servers per million inhabitants

Note: *Countries that had the highest rate of diffusion of secure servers – servers encrypted for the security of transactions online – in July 1999 have also had the highest increase in new secure servers since then. Countries with unmetered access (Australia, Canada, New Zealand and the United States) are among those with the highest penetration of secure servers, implying a greater diffusion of electronic commerce.*
Source: OECD and Netcraft *(www.netcraft.com).*

government. Progress is being made, but concerns remain, for example, over divulging sensitive private information, such as customer databases, over the Internet, or ensuring that transactions across the Internet are safe from fraud, malicious hacking and other criminal acts. Authentication and certification mechanisms are being developed to help identify users and safeguard business transactions. If e-commerce is to be an important way of doing business in the future, it will have to be reliable, secure and safe to use under all conditions. Electronic commerce and ICT also creates new challenges to policy (Box II.2), including challenges to traditional consumer laws and practices, such as in the area of taxation of goods and services, or consumer rights in the event of receiving defective goods.[4]

Some of the slowness to do business (personal or otherwise) via the Internet is to do with attitudes. Governments can help to change these by using ICT applications

Box II.2. **New policy challenges due to ICT**

Every period of radical technological change brings its new challenges and adjusting to ICT is no exception. If anything, as economic and social changes are likely to continue in the years ahead as new technologies come on stream, regulations and policies will have to be kept flexible to adjust to new circumstances. It is too early to say precisely what impact ICT will have on competition and competition policy, intellectual property rights (IPR), trade or taxation, for example. But informed judgements can be made.

First, consider competition policy. On the one hand, ICT could have pro-competitive effects by reducing search costs and thus improving market transparency, or by helping to create a truly global market place. On the other hand, the Web might lead some firms to collude in such a way as to limit competition (OECD, 2001d). Moreover, the Web may be characterised by strong network effects, where a single firm could come to dominate the network and establish a monopoly over certain lines of business. This is not necessarily a problem, as some degree of monopoly is normal in markets with a very high rate of innovation. The market should eventually break such monopolies as alternative networks develop, new innovations kick in or consumer tastes shift. Nevertheless, firms can be deft and competition policy authorities should be vigilant to ensure that such dominance does not arise except where it is the most efficient market solution.

Governments have a key role to play in the protection of IPR (see also Chapter III). The Internet makes it possible to copy and distribute any type of digital information, such as books, music, video and software, immediately and at zero or very low marginal costs. These possibilities may require some rethinking of existing IPR regimes, as they run the risk of dissuading firms from innovating. Many creators of digital information, or content, are seeking stronger legislation and enforcement of IPR. The policy response to this issue is not yet clear. For a start, stronger legislation might limit the spread of information to libraries with weak purchasing power for instance. And it is not clear to what extent these companies actually suffer from the infringement on copyright; indeed, stronger legislation might do little more than increase their profits. In any case, the main problem may not be so much about new legislation, but about enforceability; each computer linked to the Internet has the potential to distribute unlawful copies. Technology and the market may also provide its own self-regulating answers, such as CD-ROMs that are more difficult to copy.

ICT also raises challenges for trade policy. E-commerce, for example, blurs the geographical boundaries of place of supply and residence, which are key to determining jurisdiction and tariff revenue rights. And it blurs other differences too. Take a book, for instance, which is a good in the physical world; oddly, there is no

---

Box II.2. **New policy challenges due to ICT** (*cont.*)

agreement on whether a book is a good or a service when it is downloaded via the Internet. Work is underway to address these issues, particularly at WTO.

Electronic commerce raises an important challenge for tax policy, namely that of establishing a fiscal environment which businesses have faith in, while not undermining the ability of governments to raise revenues for public goods and services. OECD ministers agreed Taxation Framework Conditions in 1998, which set out the taxation principles that should apply to electronic commerce. Since then, considerable progress has been made; a consensus has emerged on how to interpret permanent establishment rules that are fundamental in deciding where profits on the conduct of e-commerce can be taxed. Progress has also been achieved in identifying pragmatic ways of achieving effective taxation in the place of consumption. And governments have also reached agreement on the main challenges and opportunities for tax administrations. More progress is needed though, notably on improving international co-ordination and co-operation.

---

themselves. Tendering public services, information, collecting taxes or procuring goods and services online can help increase government efficiency while having the additional benefit of building public confidence. In Italy, the government aims to have all income tax declarations filed on-line in 2001, greatly facilitating the processing of these forms and their transfer to other parties.

II.4. Developing a strong ICT production sector is no panacea

Should countries aim to build up their ICT sectors? Not necessarily. True, some OECD countries that have a large ICT-producing sector, such as Ireland and Finland, have benefited from rapid technological progress in this sector (Figure II.7). Having a strong ICT sector may help firms that wish to use ICT, since their close co-operation might have advantages when developing technologies for specific purposes. By definition, having a strong ICT sector should generate the skills and competencies needed to benefit from ICT use. And it should also lead to spin-offs, as in the case of Silicon Valley or in other high technology clusters.

But having an ICT sector may not be a prerequisite for growth based on new technology for three reasons. First, proximity to hardware producers may not be as

Figure II.7. **A large ICT hardware sector does not guarantee rapid MFP growth**

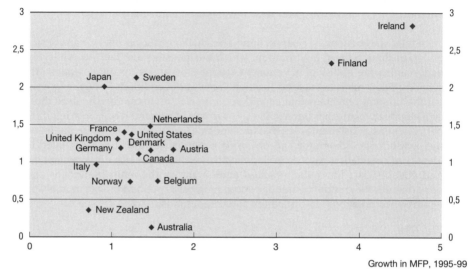

Share of ICT manufacturing in business value added, 1998 (in %)

Growth in MFP, 1995-99

Note: ICT manufacturing was almost 3 per cent of business sector value-added in Ireland and over 2 per cent in Finland, both countries where MFP grew rapidly in the second half of the 1990s. But Australia, Canada and Denmark also experienced strong MFP growth, while having only a small ICT manufacturing sector. Japan, on the other hand, has a large ICT manufacturing sector, but very low MFP growth over the 1995-99 period.

Source: MFP from OECD; OECD (2000a).

important for ICT users as proximity to software producers and service providers, which are useful to firms needing skills and advice to implement ICT-related changes. Second, much of the production of ICT hardware is highly concentrated, because of its large economies of scale and high entry costs: establishing a new semi-conductor plant cost some USD 100 million in the early 1980s, but as much as USD 1.2 billion in 1999 (United States Council of Economic Advisors, 2001).[5] In other words, a hardware sector cannot simply be set up, and only a few countries will have the necessary comparative advantages to succeed in it. The third, and most compelling, point is that several countries characterised by high ICT investment and use, as well as high MFP growth, do not have a large ICT sector. And one or two other countries that do have a large ICT sector have not been among the high growth countries of the 1990s. In sum, governments should resist believing that deliberately developing an ICT manufacturing sector would be a sure route to improved economic growth.

Key policy recommendations

While it is important to resist hype when talking about new technologies, **ICT** is an enabling technology that is transforming economic activity. Governments should take it seriously as a harbinger of growth and economic change:

- *Focus policy efforts on increasing the use of new technology*: Having an ICT sector can support growth, but is not a prerequisite. Developing an ICT manufacturing sector is costly and would not necessarily lead to faster economic growth. What counts more is how ICT is used to improve productivity and innovation.

- *Increase competition and continue with regulatory reform in the telecommunications industry to enhance the uptake of* ICT: Improving the conditions of access to local communication infrastructures is particularly important, and will require effective policies to unbundle the local loop and establish interconnection frameworks. Such policies will also help enhance access to high-speed communication services.

- *Ensure sufficient competition in hardware and software to lower costs*: Effective competition policy frameworks, lower barriers to international trade and investment, and national and international IPR regimes are important in this context.

- *Build confidence in the use of* ICT *for business and consumers*: Governments need to continue working with business and civil society, and provide guidance, to establish flexible regulatory frameworks for privacy, security and consumer protection, so that ICT applications, such as the Internet, become safe and reliable to use.

- *Make e-government a priority*: Tendering public services, collecting taxes or procuring goods online can increase government efficiency while building public confidence in ICT applications.

Notes

1. While not necessarily demonstrating a causal relationship, countries with a high relative price level of ICT investment tend to have a lower degree of competition, as measured by indicators of the level of economic regulation (Nicoletti, Scarpetta and Boylaud, 1999). Statistical tests suggest that the relationship is significant: correlation coefficient = 0.57, t-statistic = 3.07.

2. This may be linked to ongoing liberalisation of trade and investment in the OECD area (see Chapter VI).

3. One way towards such reform is "shared access", where new entrants use some of the lines of incumbent firms.

4. OECD work covers many of these issues. See *http://www.oecd.org/subject/e_commerce/*

5. And those parts of ICT hardware production that can easily be set up, such as the assembly of PCs, are likely to have less technological spin-offs than the high-tech production of semi-conductors.

Chapter III.

Harnessing the Potential
of Innovation
and Technology Diffusion

III.1. The importance of innovation

Innovation and technology diffusion are important to economic growth (OECD, 2000*f*). But their role has changed in recent years. Increased competition and globalisation has spurred a greater market orientation of funding, resulting in strong growth of business R&D, and scientific research now has a direct impact on innovation in key areas such as biotechnology and ICT (OECD, 2000*g*). ICT has also played a role, by accelerating the process of knowledge creation; the mapping of the human genome would not have been possible without modern computing technologies. It has also enabled faster networking, and made science more efficient. But despite globalisation, growing competition and the diffusion of ICT, the degree of innovation differs considerably across countries (Figure III.1).

In addition, while expenditure on innovation has risen in several OECD countries over the past decade, only few have experienced higher growth in MFP (Figure III.2). OECD work shows that R&D is an important driver of MFP (Guellec and Van Pottelsberghe, 2001). Foreign R&D is particularly important for most OECD countries (the United States being an exception), since the bulk of innovation and technological change in small countries is based on R&D that is performed abroad. But domestic R&D, *i.e.* business, government and university research, is also an important driver of MFP growth. It is also key in tapping into foreign knowledge; countries that invest in their own R&D benefit most from foreign R&D. The important role of R&D in MFP growth and the rise in R&D spending suggests that there may be unexploited potential for improved growth performance in many OECD countries.

To help realise that potential, policy has a key role to play in ensuring that new innovations continue to develop and that they are diffused throughout the economy. Governments can help in four main ways: by establishing the right incentives for

Figure III.1. **Innovation differs between OECD countries**

Patents granted at the US Patents and Trademark Office relative to GDP,
by country of inventor, 1999

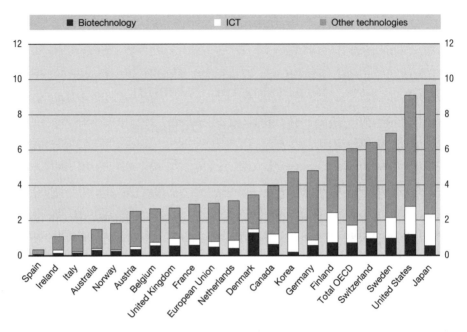

Note: The graph shows the patenting in the US market – the largest market for innovation – by inventors (firms,
        universities, laboratories, etc.) from different countries, relative to the size of each economy in terms of
        GDP. Japan, the United States, Sweden, Switzerland and Finland, patent most relative to GDP. A
        considerable part of the patenting is in ICT and biotechnology. Patents are only a partial indicator of
        innovation. Many innovations are protected by other regimes of intellectual property rights, such as
        copyrights and trademarks, while others are protected by secrecy or first-to-market strategies. Countries
        with high growth in multi-factor productivity in the 1990s have typically had high growth in patenting.
Source: OECD, based on data from the US Patent and Trademark Office.

innovation, by ensuring the generation of new knowledge, by making their own
investment in innovation more effective, and by improving interaction between the
main actors in the innovation system, that is to say, universities, research institutes
and firms.

III.2. Creating incentives for innovation

Business surveys show that firms invest in innovation because they want to gain
market share, reduce costs and increase profits.[1] Innovation has become a must for
many firms as consumer demand has become more sophisticated and competition

Figure III.2. **Increased R&D goes hand-in-hand with MFP growth**

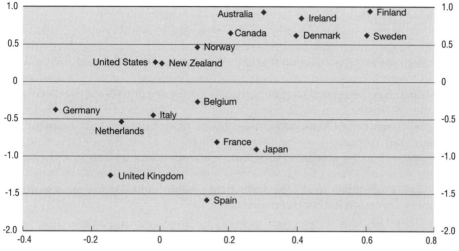

Change in MFP growth corrected for hours worked

Change in average intensity of business R&D, 1980s to 1990s

Note: OECD countries where business expenditure on R&D relative to GDP has increased most from the 1980s
         to the 1990s (the countries grouped in and around the top right-hand quartile) have typically seen the
         largest increase in MFP growth. But some countries with increased expenditure on R&D have seen no
         improvement in MFP, indicating that other factors matter. Statistical tests suggest a significant relationship
         between the two variables: correlation coefficient = 0.57, t-statistic = 2.65.
Source: Figure I.5 and OECD Main Science and Technology Indicators 2000-II.

has grown. There are several factors that influence a firm's decision to invest in innovation. Access to skills and finance are clearly important, and these are discussed later. But the decision to innovate also depends on the possible protection of the intellectual property rights (IPR) arising from research. Firms may not always use IPR to extract returns from innovation. Being first to the market may be sufficient to make high profits and other strategies, such as trade secrets or economies of scale or scope, may also be effective. But in certain new and growing industries, IPR is an important incentive too. In industries where several firms share knowledge to innovate, for example, it is important for firms to delineate their own IPR from that of others. And in areas that rely heavily on public research, such as biotechnology, firms also increasingly wish to extract their own IPR. The role of IPR has thus grown in recent years and is particularly important for new technologies.

IPR regimes are typically intended to strike a balance between ensuring sufficient private returns to investment, *e.g.* through licensing, and the diffusion of new inventions. Patent legislation, for example, grants a temporary monopoly on the use of an invention,

_43|_

but forces the inventor to make public the invention. Over the past decades, IPR regimes world-wide have been modernised, harmonised and strengthened, primarily through the adoption of the WTO's TRIPs Agreement.[2] The possible creation of a European community patent would be a further step towards harmonisation.

The major concern that has been raised in recent years regarding developments in IPR regimes is the accusation that they may have extended too far, into publicly funded research, undermining the accumulation of basic, or fundamental, knowledge. Basic research is the seed of scientific progress. Giving one firm (or a university) control over the IPR arising from basic research limits the diffusion of new knowledge and also gives large competitive advantages to the firm or university in question. The problem with excessively strong IPR regimes is that they can threaten the sharing of information, hurting scientific progress, innovation and growth in the process. Policymakers are aware of this, as witness a joint US/UK declaration in March 2000 encouraging scientists to diffuse their data on the human genome as widely as possible to promote further discovery.

Pressures to extend IPR regimes into basic research are growing as universities seek more protection for their results and as private firms realise that certain types of long-term technological research can bring large commercial pay-offs. IPR regimes must continue to provide sufficient incentives for innovation, but allow for the diffusion of fundamental knowledge too. There is no simple solution to these contradictions. Striking a balance for future innovation will require international co-operation, for although IPR regimes have been harmonised more than in the past thanks to TRIPs, they continue to differ across OECD countries, causing uncertainty in the private sector and possibly affecting innovation.

III.3. Ensuring the generation of new knowledge

Markets are beneficial, but the growing market orientation of innovation could paradoxically limit investment in basic and long-term research. Business-funded R&D has gained in importance relative to government-funded R&D over the past years (Figure III.3; OECD, 2000h), and venture capital has become a major source of funding for new innovative firms (see Chapter V). Even publicly funded research carried out in universities and public laboratories has become more commercially oriented. This may be good for innovation in the short term, but could compromise basic research and long-term innovation. Some private firms have increased their investment in this type of research in recent years, though only in specific areas with potential commercial returns. In the United States, private funding accounted for about 25 per cent of total investment in basic research in 1998. This is considerably more than in most other OECD countries.

Figure III.3. **Business R&D has risen, government R&D budgets have declined**

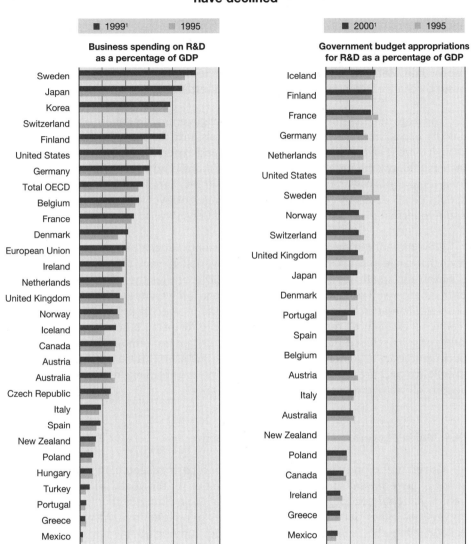

Note: Business R&D has increased considerably in several OECD countries in recent years, particularly in Finland, Japan, Sweden and the United States. Government budgets for R&D have declined relative to GDP in most OECD countries, though they increased in Belgium, Japan, Portugal and Spain.
1. Or latest available year. See source for detail.
Source: OECD, Main Science and Technology Indicators, December 2000.

In practice, governments must fund the bulk of basic and high-risk research. One reason is the lack of direct, short-term, commercial applications. And, as discussed above, the outcomes of basic research are typically not covered by IPR regimes, making it less attractive for private firms to invest. This kind of research typically also has a long time horizon and carries high risks, which only a few large corporations can assume. Moreover, a large number of scientific discoveries and lucrative inventions occur by chance, often as the by-product of interdisciplinary work.

The large uncertainties involved imply that governments cannot always link their funding for basic research to precise scientific goals. Take the example of particle physics: though there is an acceptance that using giant and expensive particle accelerators will increase the overall understanding of matter, there is no common view on what the long-term applications of any discoveries will be. Funding for scientific research should be allocated by competitive procedures, however, with scientific excellence and intellectual merit set as the primary conditions (Branscomb, 1999).

Governments in most OECD countries cannot fund all fields of research to a level that can lead to important scientific discoveries. In many, the volume of spending is simply too small. A growing number of OECD countries therefore co-operate with each other, as well as complementing institutional (university and laboratory) funding of scientific research with more focused efforts in specific fields, aiming to create "centres of excellence". Austria's Kplus programme, for instance, supports competitively selected joint science-industry research centres that perform high-quality research. Such centres are important to achieve the scale and scope that is needed for scientific excellence and are also important in building the research networks needed to absorb knowledge and technology from abroad.

III.4. Making government funding more effective

Government funding typically goes beyond basic research. In practice, a large share of government funded R&D aims to meet public goals, such as improved health, national security and a clean environment. Some of this funding goes to universities, other parts to public laboratories or private firms. Although achieving economic benefits is not the prime aim of such funding, it may have large indirect impacts on growth. For instance, US funding for the National Institutes of Health has been an important driver of the current boom in biotechnology. And R&D funding from the US Department of Defense has contributed to many important innovations in ICT, including the Internet and artificial intelligence. Such funding has sometimes served vested interests, however, with low economic or social benefits. Governments need to ensure that they have sufficient flexibility in orienting funding towards areas with high potential benefits, *i.e.* those that push the technological frontier or generate new knowledge. Competitive funding of universities and public laboratories, in particular, is of great importance.

Apart from science and high-risk research, most OECD governments encourage R&D and innovation in the private sector. Such support typically takes the form of grants, subsidies, loans or tax credits. And as Figure III.4 shows, there are large cross-country differences in the scale of such support.[3] Direct support instruments, such as grants, are more selective and can potentially be channelled to areas with high potential returns in a way that tax credits cannot. Empirical research of such programmes provides a few lessons (Guellec and Van Pottelsberghe, 2000). First, government support does lead to additional private funding, although there is also some crowding out. Second, the level of funding is important: a low level has only little impact on overall business funding, whereas a high level substitutes for private R&D. Support for defence R&D, in particular, crowds out civilian R&D in the business sector. Third, support is more effective in generating additional private funding if policies are relatively stable over time. And finally, the interaction between the different types of support is important.

Supporting business R&D can be expensive and governments should continually monitor the costs of such support against the would-be benefits. In principle, government should support innovation in areas where there are large spill-overs and where the private sector would not get involved on its own (Stiglitz, 1999). Public-private partnerships can help to share risks and costs and may increase the leverage of government funding. Competitive procedures are important in implementing such partnerships while the use of consortia may prevent governments from only supporting one firm as the "winner". Governments should be vigilant against serving vested interests, however. Support programmes can lead to the growth of powerful lobbies with an interest in prolonging support, even after the social returns of those programmes have disappeared. Governments should also not crowd out new sources of private finance aimed at innovation, such as venture capital (see Chapter V).

Another question for policy makers is whether they should be concerned over free riding. Knowledge, especially that arising from public research, is increasingly global and accessible, which means that firms or countries can benefit from research carried out elsewhere without contributing to costs. This should not deter governments from funding research. First, the evidence suggests that free riding is not a real option. In several small and successful economies, *e.g.* Finland, investment in public and private research has increased in recent years. Countries need their own R&D to understand and absorb knowledge developed abroad, to become part of innovation networks, and to develop their own skills. Moreover, R&D can give first-mover advantages. Free riding is also an inevitable consequence of the non-proprietary character of fundamental knowledge. Any excessive free riding – where it exists – can be reduced by sharing the costs of large scientific projects internationally.

47

Figure III.4. **Direct and indirect government support for R&D, 1999**

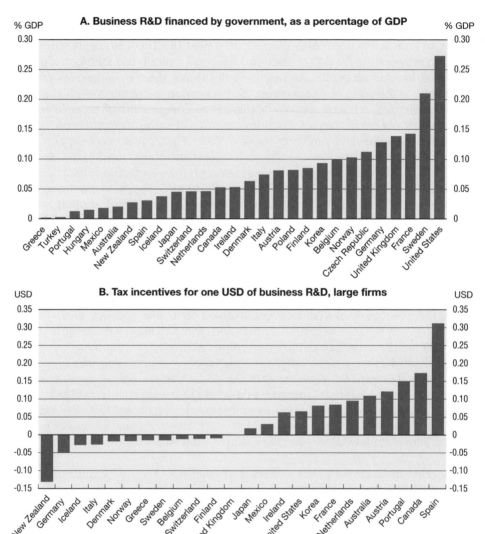

Note: The top graph shows that government-financed business R&D is greatest in the United States, at nearly
0.3 per cent of GDP. The four OECD countries with the largest direct support for R&D (United States,
Sweden, France and the United Kingdom) all have large R&D defence programmes that are partially
contracted out to the business sector. The second graph shows the after-tax benefit of investing in R&D,
accounting for all available tax incentives (see Guellec and Van Pottelsberghe, 2000, for details). In terms
of providing tax incentives as encouragement for R&D, Spain is the most generous country and New
Zealand the least. In the United Kingdom, the tax treatment in 1999 was effectively neutral with respect to
R&D. Data are for 1999, or the latest year available.
Source: OECD (2000h); OECD Main Science and Technology Indicators 2000-II.

III.5. Strengthening interaction within the innovation system

Interaction within the innovation system, notably between science and industry, has grown in recent years. Indeed, a recent analysis of US biotechnology patents found that more than 70 per cent of citations were to papers originating solely in public science institutions (McMillan *et al.*, 2000). This change shows the growing interest of the business sector in scientific research and the researchers, technologies, methods and instruments that come with it. Nevertheless, there are considerable differences among OECD countries in the extent to which innovation draws on science. The

Figure III.5. **Science-innovation links have developed rapidly
in some OECD countries**

Average number of scientific papers cited in patents taken in the United States,
by country of origin

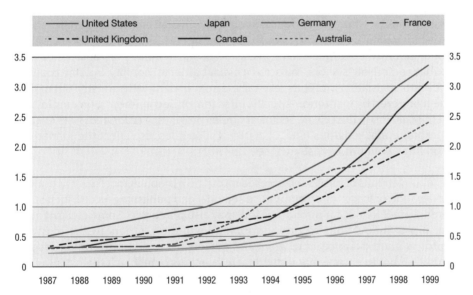

Note: The graph shows that patents increasingly cite the findings of scientific research as an important
ingredient for new innovations. This is the case in most areas of scientific research, but particularly in
biochemistry, organic chemistry and medical research. The overall pattern in the graph changes very little
if biochemistry and pharmaceutical patents are excluded. Differences in patent specialisation therefore do
not explain the cross country differences. In the United States, Canada and Australia, innovation draws
more strongly on scientific research than in France, Germany and Japan. Language is not the explanation
for these differences; innovation in non-English speaking countries such as Finland, the Netherlands and
Sweden also draws increasingly on scientific research carried out inside the country. The graph is based
on US patents, since the estimates are not available for European and Japanese patents.

Source: CHI Research, *http://www.chiresearch.com*; see also OECD (2001e).   49 growth in science-industry links over the 1990s, as measured by patent citations has been much more rapid in the United States, Canada, the United Kingdom and Australia than in France, Germany or Japan (Figure III.5).

Policy helps explain these cross-country differences. In the United States, for example, the linkages have been strengthened by initiatives in the 1980s and 1990s, like the extension of patent protection to publicly funded research (Jaffe, 1999), and the introduction of co-operative research and development agreements (CRADAs) to facilitate technology transfer from the public sector to private industry. Of course, the success of these initiatives was helped by the growing interest in scientific research on the part of the business sector (Mowery and Ziedonis, 2000).

Many OECD countries have followed the US example (OECD, 2000*h*; 2001*e*). But several barriers still impede the flow of knowledge between science and industry. There is not enough mobility of researchers in some countries for a start. In the United States, scientists and engineers change employer every four years, and even more frequently in areas such as software and ICT. But in Japan, only 20 per cent of engineers change employer in their entire career. Overall employment rules and job market constraints are partly to blame (see Chapter IV), as are international barriers to labour mobility. But other factors, like a lack of transferability of pensions between the public and private sectors, can act as a major barrier to mobility. In some countries, public sector legislation prohibits researchers from working with industry. But mobility can be hampered by institution-specific rules too, on secondments, on employment in a secondary job in the private sector, and rules preventing academics from engaging in entrepreneurial activities (OECD, 2001*e*). These rules also affect the formation of spin-off firms from public research (see Box III.1).

The conventions of public sector research can be a problem too. Faculty promotion and evaluation practices often emphasise seniority and publishing record, for instance. Differences in IPR rules for public research may also play a role. Some countries grant ownership of innovations to the performing institution, others to the individual inventor. A good practice is to grant IPR ownership to the performing research organisation but to ensure that individual researchers or research teams enjoy a fair share of resulting royalties. Increased links between science and industry are needed in many OECD countries, but policy makers should also be aware of the risks. Too much commercialisation of universities, for example, may reduce the quality of scientific research and education.

Apart from links between science and industry, co-operation between firms has also increased, both domestically and globally. Firms engage in these co-operative arrangements for various reasons. First, the cost of major innovations, such as a new generation of semiconductors, is often beyond the means of any single firm. Second,

Box III.1. **Spin-offs from publicly funded research**

Spin-offs of public research are but one example of the interaction between science and industry. Out of the 1000 most profitable firms in Canada in 2000, seven started their life in 1998 as a university spin-off. While modest in number compared with the overall creation of new firms, spin-offs are an important element in the interaction between science and industry. Most are concentrated in ICT and biotechnology. Spin-off formation is rising across the OECD, but it is about three to four times higher in North America than elsewhere (Figure III.6). Spin-off formation in the United States, Canada and France seems closely linked to overall start-up rates, but the overall conditions for entrepreneurship do not fully explain the differences. Countries such as Finland and Germany seem to create more spin-offs from public research than one would expect from their low start-up rates (OECD, 2001e).

Figure III.6. **Spin-offs from publicly funded research**
Per billion USD of government R&D

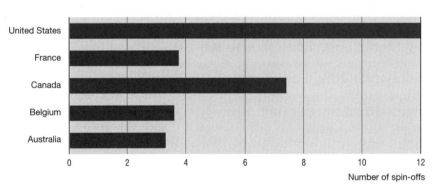

Note: The US leads in the number of spin-off firms created by publicly funded research organisations (United States and Canada: universities only) per USD of publicly funded R&D. Data as follows: Australia, 1991-99; Belgium, 1990-99; Canada: 1990-98; France: 1992-99; United States: 1994-98.
Source: OECD (2001e).

highly skilled researchers are scarce and firms may want to share these resources. Third, some key technological developments, including biotechnology, cross traditional scientific and firm boundaries, and thus require co-operation (Rycroft and Kash, 1999). Fourth, co-operation reduces duplication of research and thus improves efficiency. And fifth, co-operation may enable the development of technological standards. Standards are needed to establish a large enough market, which is often the only way to recover high development costs. For example, the development of the GSM standard has provided a strong impetus for the development of mobile telephony in Europe.

Such collaboration is good, but raises several policy issues. First, it may run counter to objectives to deepen competition for innovation (see Box in Chapter II). Certain OECD governments currently permit (and sometimes encourage) co-operation in the pre-competitive stages of research – when research is not yet commercially applicable – but combine this with vigilant competition policy to limit anti-competitive conduct. The US National Cooperative Research Act of 1984, for instance, established a "rule of reason" for evaluating the competition policy implications of joint ventures in pre-competitive research, reducing the risks of sanctions for firms in engaging in such activities.

Second, international sources of knowledge are increasingly important for innovation and co-operation increasingly takes place across national borders. To support this, governments have to encourage openness to foreign sources of innovation and revisit older policies that might have aimed at fostering national champions or achieving self-sufficiency in scientific and technological know-how.

Collaboration between firms helps not only to transfer knowledge, but technologies too. Specific policies may be needed to strengthen this process. For instance, would-be users may simply be unaware of a technology's existence, or may be waiting for others to use it first. Governments can help to overcome such information barriers and encourage the process of learning-by-doing. After all, only by deploying a new technology will its usage and benefits spread and networks develop.

Key policy recommendations

Overall, policymakers should look beyond the current wave of technological change and seek to foster the kind of **innovative environment** in which new growth can flourish:

- *Give greater priority to basic research; future innovation will be jeopardised without it*: Such funding should be competitive and emphasise scientific excellence and merit as key criteria.

- *Improve the effectiveness of government funding for innovation*: Government funding needs to focus on areas with high economic or social benefits, not vested interests. Public-private partnerships can help to share costs and may increase

Key policy recommendations (*cont.*)

the leverage of government funding. Competitive procedures are important for such partnerships while the use of consortia may avoid that governments only support one firm as the "winner".

- *Make greater use of competitive funding and evaluation in supporting public research*: Support for institutions remains important, but competitive funding instruments and strong evaluation are needed to improve the quality of research and focus on the areas of greatest value.

- *Tackle new challenges in intellectual property regimes*: Governments should ensure that IPR regimes governing publicly funded research strike a balance between the diffusion of knowledge across research institutions and its application by the private sector. Striking this balance will require international co-operation.

- *Remove barriers and regulations that limit effective interaction between universities, firms and public laboratories*: To augment the flow of knowledge and workers between science and industry, governments should review rules and regulations that limit the mobility of public sector researchers or restrict institutional links between public and private sector organisations. Ensure greater openness to foreign sources of knowledge.

Notes

1. Firms are not the only party requiring the right incentives to innovate. Incentives for public researchers, universities and public research laboratories are discussed below.

2. TRIPs has imposed minimum standards of protection to a broad range of IPR regimes, and has extended IPR protection to technologies like micro-organisms, plant genetic material and computer programmes. Under TRIPs, protection offered has to be enforceable within a country, while IP disputes between countries can be taken up by the WTO's Dispute Settlement Body as a trade complaint. The TRIPs agreement has considerably reduced the cross-country differences in IPR regimes in the OECD.

3. The costs to government of R&D tax credits are only available for some countries. In Australia and Canada, the bulk of government support for business R&D is provided through R&D tax credits. In France, Japan and the United States, R&D tax credits play only a minor role in overall government support for business R&D.

Chapter IV.

Enhancing Human Capital and Realising its Potential

IV.1. Renewed emphasis on human capital as an engine of growth

The role of human capital as a central pillar of the development process is not new. There is a well-established relationship between human capital, understood as the skills and competencies embodied in workers, and labour productivity – and it is not surprising that improvements in one should lead to increases in the other. Consequently, as empirical studies have found, human capital is a significant determinant of economic growth.[1]

There is, however, renewed interest in the productivity-enhancing role of human capital. One reason is its complementarity with new technology: for ICT to be developed and used effectively, and network externalities of new technology to materialise, the right skills and competencies must be in place. One of the factors behind the good growth record of some countries has been the availability of a large pool of qualified personnel. And skilled labour shortages are rightly considered as a constraint to the growth process. This is why, increasingly, some OECD countries use foreign labour to fill in shortages of qualified personnel. For example, in the United States, foreign workers filled more than a quarter of qualified ICT-jobs created during 1996-1998.

The result is that the demand for "knowledge-intensive" employment has risen considerably (Figure IV.1). During the 1990s, in the OECD countries for which data are available, the rise in the number of knowledge workers (scientists, engineers and others, *e.g.* ICT specialists and technicians that generate knowledge), accounted for nearly 30 per cent of the net employment gains recorded during this period. Wages have followed a similar pattern. For example in the United States, the wage of knowledge workers has risen much faster than wages of other occupations. Between 1985 and 1998, real earnings of knowledge-intensive workers grew by almost 17 per cent, cumulatively, compared with 5 1/4 per cent for the average US employee. During the same period "goods-producing" occupations suffered a cut in their real earnings of nearly 2 1/2 per cent.

55

Figure IV.1. **The rising importance of knowledge-intensive employment**

Employment growth by group of occupations in selected OECD countries, average annual percentage change, 1992-1999

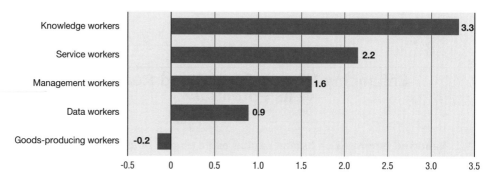

Note: There is a skill-bias in job creation. In all OECD countries considered in the Figure (the United States and EU countries), knowledge-intensive employment has grown much faster than other types of employment. In addition, there is some evidence (not shown in the Figure) for the United States that knowledge workers have enjoyed a sizeable rise in their real pay. By contrast, goods-producing workers have suffered lower employment and a cut in their real wages.

Source: OECD (2001f).

IV.2. Strengthening education and training systems

To take advantage of the growth potential of new technology, it is essential to intensify efforts to upgrade human capital. Policies have to ensure that formal education systems respond to changing requirements in a cost-effective way. But education policies, important as they are, need to be supplemented with action in the area of adult learning. A coherent life-long learning strategy is therefore required, as reiterated by OECD Education Ministers at their meeting of April 2001.

Ensuring a solid foundation in basic education

In the knowledge-based economy, providing everyone with at least a basic educational background has become more important. To be employable and productive, young people must be equipped with at least upper secondary education (or an apprenticeship certificate). In recent years, completion rates of upper secondary education have increased in all OECD countries. Still, more has to be done since completion rates vary considerably across the OECD area (Figure IV.2). In many countries, more than a fifth of every youth cohort leave the formal education system without the types of skills and qualifications that are valued in the labour market.

Figure IV.2.   **Non-completion of secondary education, 1998**

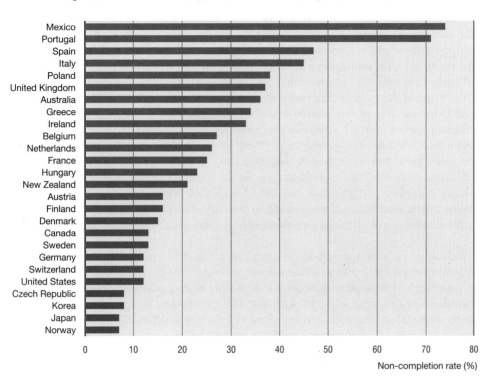

Non-completion rate (%)

Note: *Non-completion of secondary education varies significantly across countries. In the Figure, the non-completion rate is defined as the percentage of individuals aged 25 to 34 who have not attained at least upper secondary education.*
Source: OECD, *Education at a Glance*, 2000.

Early education and child care are key to reduce school under-achievement. Indeed, the bases for the skills needed in the knowledge economy, notably communication skills, are acquired early in life (OECD, 2001*g*). Policies to improve early childhood education are generally cost-effective, in that they can reduce the need for more costly interventions to remedy school failure and anti-social behaviour later on. For example, there is evidence that the US Perry Programme of early education yields substantial long-term benefits in terms of subsequent academic achievement and work opportunities, compared with the cost of the programme.[2] And while early education policies have immediate financial repercussions, they deliver positive results in the medium term.. This is why improving access to early childhood education is a policy priority that needs to be intensified in all the countries (OECD, 2001*h*).

Another reason for school under-achievement is the fact that knowledge opportunities are unevenly distributed across different socio-economic groups: the lower the educational inequalities, the better the school performance for the country as a whole (Willms, 2000). More specifically, children from disadvantaged groups have to be provided with adequate education opportunities to help reduce cross-country differences in educational attainment. The challenge is sizeable. For instance, in France, 62 per cent of the 15-year-olds coming from the poorest 20 per cent of the families have had to repeat at least one year in school compared with 17 per cent in the case of the children coming from the richest 20 per cent of the families. Education inequalities have even worsened in certain countries. Thus, in the United States, over the past two decades there has been a widening inequality in college completion between the children of low and high income groups. As the experience of some Nordic countries shows, targeted programmes can help break this "vicious circle" of educational inequalities. These programmes need to take into account the importance for school achievement of a trust-based environment and, more generally, social capital (Box IV.1).

Teacher quality appears to be a growing problem in some OECD counties. Yet, it is important for student achievement. In many OECD countries, the education system faces considerable difficulties in recruiting high-quality personnel. Recruitment problems, combined with the fact that the profession is ageing rapidly (in the European Union, more than one in five teachers will retire within a decade), has increased difficulties in adapting schools to new technology. In 1999, it is estimated that investments in ICT for education amounted to as much as USD 16 billion in the OECD area as a whole, but owing to the lack of qualified ICT educators these new investments are under-exploited. Making teaching more attractive, for both present and future teachers, becomes a more urgent policy concern in the face of teacher shortages. Attractiveness can be fostered through a better recognition of the profession and wider career opportunities. However, these measures would have to go hand-in-hand with having effective mechanisms in place to evaluate teachers.

It has also been suggested that parents be given a greater say in the choice of school for their children's education, for example through a system of vouchers. This would introduce an element of competition between schools and improve the cost-effectiveness of the system. However, these proposals have been criticised on the grounds that a vouchers' system will not raise standards, especially in low-income neighbourhoods where school choice may be limited. More attention should be given to the pros and cons of vouchers.

Adapting higher education and making it more cost-effective

Higher education is essential to innovation and technological change, especially now that the distance between research and its application is narrowing (see

---

Box IV.1. **The importance of social capital and trust**

Social networks and trust, i.e. social capital, can help realise human capital. Communities with high levels of social capital tend to achieve better school outcomes than communities which face social fragmentation and isolation.

Moreover, the success of certain inter-firm arrangements in Northern Italy, or the innovative environment prevailing in Silicon Valley can be partly explained by social capital (OECD, 2001*i*). Trust-based relations facilitate co-operation and are essential to good economic performance. If individuals trust each other, they will be more prone to exchange information and knowledge, compared with environments characterised by secrecy, self-sufficiency and territoriality. The success of Silicon Valley and failure of the Route 128 corridor outside Boston can be explained partly by differences in social capital. Guiso *et al.* (2000) argue that trust-based relations between enterprises and credit institutions in Northern Italy may lie behind a more risk-taking mentality there. In short, social capital provides the glue which facilitates co-operation, exchange and innovation.

Despite these connections, however, no clear evidence emerges from the limited research to date that social capital contributes to economic growth at national level. This could partly reflect measurement difficulties, and lack of data – social capital is commonly measured through a range of crude proxies, including trust and participation in association life.

Policy thinking on social capital is still in its infancy. This is one reason why it is such a controversial notion. Yet, while it is true that governments cannot "produce" social capital directly, they can create an environment conducive to investment in it. For example, in education and training, more attention could be given to interpersonal skills which are so often critical to trust-based relations and economic activity.

Chapter III). Higher education is also important for ensuring an adequate supply of qualified labour, and thus to sustain the growth process. Given such requirements, the links between higher education and labour markets should be strengthened. This can be achieved through a wider provision of short-cycle courses, a larger involvement of the private sector in course design, increased learning possibilities for workers who need to update their skills and the application of effective financial mechanisms.

Greater emphasis on short-cycle programmes can help improve the match between the interests of the students and the labour market. Several OECD countries are now giving priority to these programmes. In 1997, Hungary introduced a new short-cycle programme intended to have a closer link to industry than traditional university courses. Mexico's new technological universities, similar to the French vocationally-oriented university institutes (IUTs), offer two-year, applied study courses aimed at labour market needs. These experiences have been positive in terms of student quality and graduate employment.

The involvement of the private sector in higher education provision provides another occupationally-oriented option. Some countries, France and Finland for instance, encourage the public-private partnerships for the financing of programmes and the design of curricula. In other countries, such as Japan, Korea and the United States, the private involvement in the provision of higher education is already large. The involvement of companies like Microsoft, Sun Microsystems and Cisco in the provision of ICT-related education is now well-established. At the same time, however, governments must ensure adequate provision in fields of wider importance for society such as humanities and certain branches of science.

One way to strengthen the economic effectiveness of education is to improve the school-to-work transition in order to motivate students, and increase their employment prospects. Such combinations have been common for many years in countries with strong apprenticeship traditions such as Germany and Switzerland. During the 1990s, Norway strengthened its apprenticeship system to encourage higher participation by young people, including through the restructuring of training wages and of financial incentives for employers. In some countries where apprenticeship traditions have traditionally been weak – such as Australia, Canada and Sweden – programmes have been introduced in the 1990s to better combine formal education with workplace experience.

To help update workers' skills, higher education could be made more "adult friendly". Already in the United States, almost half of the student population consists of mature and part-time adult students, a dramatic shift from the previous generation. The Australian technical and further education colleges provides an interesting example which could perhaps be emulated in other countries. The system is flexible – for instance it is possible to study part-time, at distance and on week ends. Access requirements take into account not only former education qualifications but also work experience. The result is that, in Australia, 12 per cent of enrolees in the formal education system are aged 35 and over, which is three times the OECD average (Figure IV.3). In all countries, new technology can be better exploited to widen the learning opportunities of adults.

Upward pressures in public spending on education should be accompanied with a stronger emphasis on reinforcing the incentives for improving education outcomes, i.e. making the system more cost-effective. For example, as Figure IV.4 shows, countries

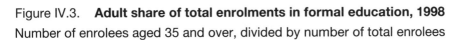

Figure IV.3. **Adult share of total enrolments in formal education, 1998**

Number of enrolees aged 35 and over, divided by number of total enrolees

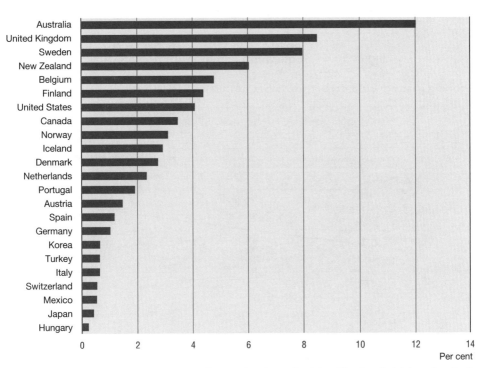

Note: *Relatively few workers have access to formal education and training. The share in total enrolments of adults aged 35 and over who participate in either secondary or tertiary education is low.*

Source: OECD (2001*g*).

like Canada, Finland and the Netherlands achieve a relatively high level of literacy, while their education budgets as a per cent of GDP are no higher than the OECD average. Subsidising institutions on the basis of their performance would introduce a healthy element of competition and probably improve school achievement. But this raises equity concerns, as well as a risk of "creaming" – which arises when education institutions tend to enrol students who are likely to complete the courses successfully, rather than those whose initial qualifications are far from the course objectives (OECD, 2000*h*). In addition, it is advisable to delegate budgetary powers to the institutions to allow them to allocate the funds in the most efficient way, provided that managing the business side of education does not distract from actual teaching. The Danish "taximeter" system provides an innovative example of a performance-based financial strategy. Under this system, the subsidy which is

61

provided to learning institutions depends directly on student performance. Institutions can thus retain part of the profits (the difference between taximeter rates and actual costs of education); but they have to bear part of the losses they incur.

Figure IV.4. **Education expenditure and literacy**

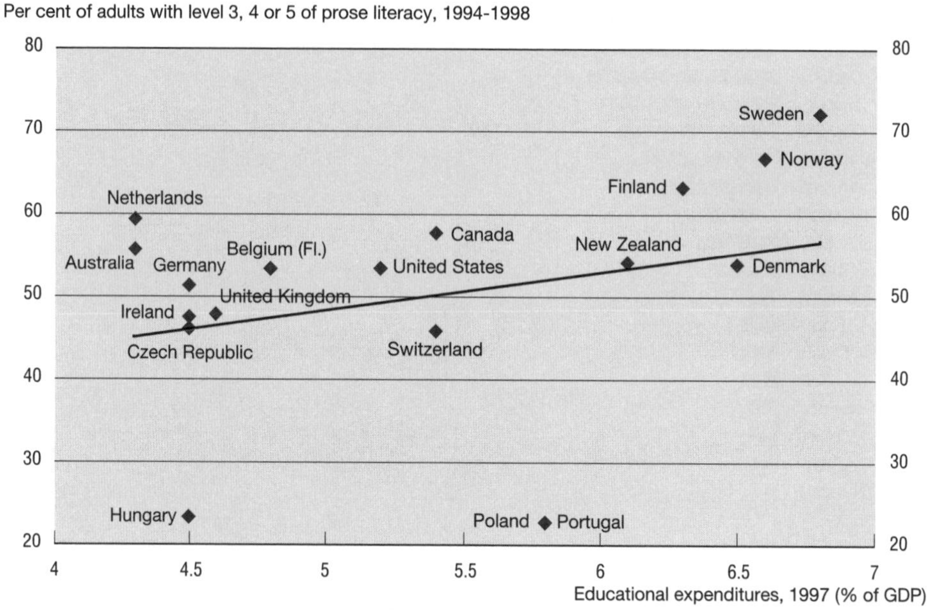

Per cent of adults with level 3, 4 or 5 of prose literacy, 1994-1998

Note: *Spending more does not necessarily improve literacy. The countries that lie above the line have a relatively good literacy performance, for a given level of education expenditure.*
Source: OECD, *Education at a Glance*, 2000 and OECD, *Literacy in the Information Age*, 2000.

Strengthening the incentive to invest in training and adult learning

There is widespread agreement that incentives for adult learning, *e.g.* via direct public expenditure or tax exemption, are insufficient for today's requirements. About two thirds of the adult population does not receive any formal training at all. In particular, the unskilled, older workers and those on precarious forms of employment, have relatively few opportunities to learn or upgrade their skills, thereby aggravating the risk of being left behind. It is important to develop policy measures to improve the distribution of vocational training across different categories of workers. Also, the content of training needs to reflect the rising demand for "soft skills", like interpersonal and communication skills.

The problem is that firms may have weak incentives to provide on-the-job training. Employers who fear that the employee may move to another firm do not have much incentive to invest in the human capital of their workers. The result is that firms will tend to pursue a "buying strategy", seeking to recruit already skilled workers. One approach would be to bring the tax treatment of training expenses by firms closer in line with that of investment in other assets, such as R&D and software. Alternatively, allowances for the depreciation of human capital could be introduced, as is already the case with physical capital – this however would entail a change in accounting rules, which presently ignore human capital.

Individuals themselves may be reluctant to engage in training in the absence of a certification system or clear evidence that their investments in training will yield sufficiently high returns. To reduce the tendency to under-invest in training, countries should build a well-functioning system of recognition and certification of competencies. Indeed, individuals will invest more in their human capital, through either formal courses or informal learning, when the competencies which are acquired are portable in the labour market – something recognition and certification undoubtedly facilitate. The French *bilan de compétences* is an interesting recent example in this area. Another

---

Box IV.2. **An innovative experience: individual learning accounts**

If firms under-train their workers, employability becomes mainly an individual concept. Systems that encourage individuals themselves to invest in their own human capital (and rely less on the firm) must then be considered. Individual learning accounts (ILAs) provide an interesting innovation in this respect.

Like voucher schemes, ILAs are based on the principle that individuals are best placed to choose what and how they want to learn and improve their skills. The costs are also shared between the various players *i.e.* firms, individuals and governments. ILAs can provide training opportunities to groups which do not generally participate in such activities. For example, in the United Kingdom, ILAs were introduced in April 2000 as a key part of the government strategy on lifelong learning. In Sweden, ILAs are currently being piloted and refined and will probably be in place in January 2002. Similarly, in the United States, Individual Development Accounts are available to low and medium-income households.

These innovative systems are part of a new approach to welfare policies that instead of supporting income and consumption attempt to promote human capital investment and improving individual employability. They provide a promising avenue for enhancing the human capital of groups which typically receive little training.

63

interesting innovation is the development of the Computer Driving Licence introduced by Finland in 1995 as a way to certify ICT computer knowledge. This system certifies that the holder of the licence possesses basic ICT literacy and is able to use a personal computer at a basic level of competence. But a more comprehensive approach is the creation in some countries of so-called Individual Learning Accounts (ILAs) – Box IV.2.

IV.3. Adapting labour market institutions and regulations to the changing nature of work

To enhance the benefits of new technology and realise the potential of human capital, it is essential to reorganise work within firms. There is a marked association between ICT use and new work practices such as teamworking, employee involvement and flatter management structures (Figure IV.5 and Box IV.3). Moreover, during the

Figure IV.5.   **New work practices and ICT investment**

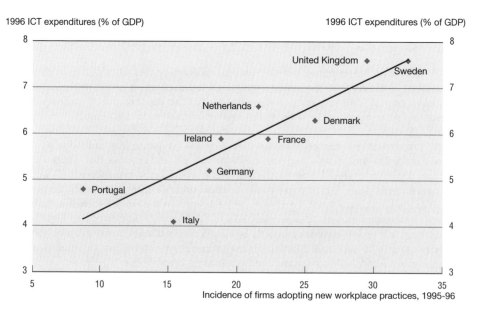

Note: ICT-penetration and work-reorganisation go hand-in-hand. In the Figure, work re-organisation is measured as the incidence of new work practices (teamwork, job rotation schemes, employee involvement, flatter management, etc.). Sweden and the United Kingdom, which have high ICT penetration, also have a high incidence of new work practices.

Source: OECD (2001f).

Box IV.3. **The changing nature of work**

OECD economies are undergoing a major process of work reorganisation with profound consequences on the nature and forms of work. In the past, workers were required to perform specialised tasks within the framework of standardised production processes. In today's economy, they are often given responsibilities in different domains, for which multiple skills and the ability to work in teams are required. These changes are associated with greater use of ICT (Table IV.1) and with better productivity performance at the firm level.

This phenomenon is reflected in the large variety of new work practices that are being implemented by firms. These include, *inter alia*, teamwork, flatter management structures, employee involvement and suggestion schemes. The common element among these practices is that they entail a greater degree of responsibility of individual workers regarding the content of their work and, to some extent, a greater proximity between management and labour. Wages and working conditions, at the same time, tend to be more flexible – in the sense that they are likely to evolve depending on the changing demand requirements. As a result, systems of performance-related pay (*e.g.* bonuses, profit-sharing schemes, stock options) are on the rise and, more generally, workers are increasingly rewarded on the basis of achievements.

A related emerging phenomenon is telework. According to a European Commission survey, there were in 1999 almost 9 million teleworkers in the European Union, accounting for 6 per cent of the total workforce. This figure includes those working at least one day a week away from the office on a regular basis, but also occasional telework. In the United States, in 1998, there were almost 16 million teleworkers (or telecommuters as defined in the relevant survey), that is 13 per cent of the workforce, while in Japan, teleworkers account for about 8 per cent of the workforce.

Table IV.1. **Work re-organisation and ICT: a close relationship**
Proportion of firms using ICT

	Among firms which reorganise work	Among firms which *do not* reorganise work
Australia	24	14
Finland	62	52
European Union		
(except Finland)	49	34
United States	58	49

Note: ICT *use among firms which reorganise work is significantly larger than is the case among firms which do not reorganise work. Owing to methodological differences in the relevant questionnaires, figures cannot be compared between countries.*
Source: OECD (2001f).

65

1990s, labour productivity in US firms which implemented ICT and reorganised work grew very rapidly while it practically stagnated in firms which implemented new technology but did not reorganise work (OECD, 2001f). Likewise, in Denmark, productivity gains in firms that introduce new work practices together with ICT are four to five times larger than in firms that introduce ICT and do not reorganise work.

Social partners and government can work together to ensure that this virtuous circle of new work practices, new technology and productivity is set in motion. This crucially depends on workers being given a sufficient "voice" in the firm. Institutions, which allow a closer contact between management and employees, can indeed help build a high-skill, high-trust enterprise climate which facilitates change. New work practices tend to be more prevalent among firms with some form of employee involvement than among other firms.

Changes in work practices also raise a number of challenges for collective bargaining. First, the rising importance of performance-based remuneration does not

Figure IV.6. **Low tenure countries tend to enjoy high productivity growth**

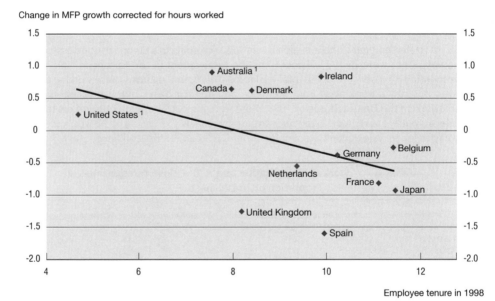

Change in MFP growth corrected for hours worked

Employee tenure in 1998

Note: Job mobility tends to be high in most of the countries where multi-factor productivity has improved during the 1990s. Conversely, job mobility tends to be low in countries where productivity has worsened. Job mobility is measured here as average employees' tenure.
1. Employee tenure data for Australia and the United States refer to 2000.
Source: OECD (2001f); MFP from Figure I.5.

fit well with traditional systems of wage formation, which are often based on rigid classifications of jobs and an excessive emphasis on seniority. This is important since performance-based remuneration is an integral part of the process of work reorganisation. Second, collective agreements and government regulations should provide for more flexibility in working hours, allowing greater scope for averaging legal requirements over the year and allowing new forms of work to flourish.

Finally, there is some evidence of increased employment mobility between firms (and not just within them as just discussed). More generally, in some of the countries where multi-factor productivity has accelerated, employment tenure tends to be low (Figure IV.6). Though the causes are not established, it is clear that a certain degree of mobility is needed to seize new business opportunities. In this regard, there is a need for adjusting employment regulations in certain countries. However, such reforms must take into account the need for creating a stable employment environment that induces firms to train their workers. After all, job instability is associated with less training.

IV.4. Bridging the digital and knowledge divides

Unequal access to new technology and to learning how to use it effectively has become a matter of major policy concern. The significance of this knowledge divide is three-fold. On the one hand, there is a risk that those without access to ICT skills and knowledge will lag further behind as technology progresses, with whole groups of society becoming less and less capable of participating in the economy. This could add pressures towards wider income inequality, potentially eroding support for growth-enhancing policies and driving up costs of social programs. Moreover, one of the main advantages of ICT lies in its network effects, so that the more people that use the system, the greater the economic benefits of the new technology. And, given the importance of human capital to growth, closing the divides should by definition improve human capital and medium-term growth potential as well.

Large segments of OECD populations do not yet have access to modern technologies. The incidence of Internet home access in rural areas, among older people and by low-income individuals and households is relatively limited. As shown in Figure IV.7, the richest 10 per cent households are 2 to 10 times more likely to have access to the Internet than is the case of the poorest 10 per cent. Policies to reduce costs and raise confidence will facilitate a wider diffusion of ICT, thereby narrowing the digital divide (see Chapter II for the policies in question). As the new technology network expands, rural areas will be in a better position to participate in the network economy. There is also an issue of a digital divide between countries, the so-called "North-South" digital divide. To address some of the problems raised by this divide,

67

G8 countries recently decided to create a digital opportunities task force (the *dot force*). Many of the policies recommended in this report will apply to developing countries as well, though most are starting from a much lower base. Moreover, development co-operation policies have a key role to play in helping developing countries to create the right policy environment to attract ICT investment and to make use of ICT as part of achieving their poverty reduction goals.

Figure IV.7. **Internet home access among households by income level**

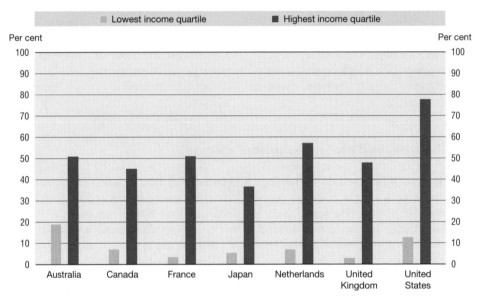

Note: *Access to the Internet is influenced by household income. Between 3 and 20 per cent of the households which belong to the lowest quartile of income have access to the Internet. This is several times less than is the case of households of high-income groups. However, the divide is narrowing: access to the Internet among low-income households is rising relatively fast.*

Source: OECD (2001), Understanding the Digital Divide.

It is not just a question of having computers. Schools and education authorities are also aware of the importance of integrating ICT into teaching and learning, both to prepare students for the information society and to make the most of new learning tools. Figure IV.8 shows that access to new technology in schools varies considerably across countries. Policymakers should encourage schools, libraries and learning centres to invest in computers and access to the Internet to enable the disadvantaged to gain access to learning and information resources at a public institution. A major impediment in this area is the shortage of qualified teachers. This is limiting the extent to which computers are effectively used in schools.

Figure IV.8. **Home and school access to computers in OECD countries**

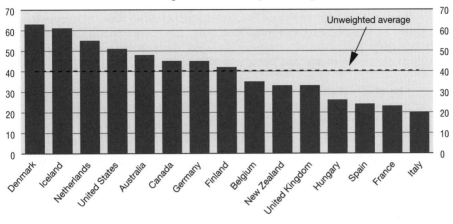

A. Percentage of households possessing a PC

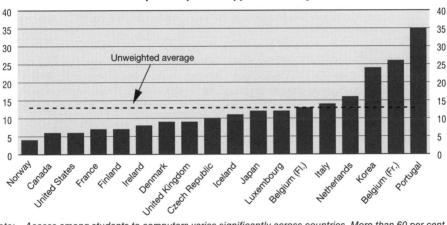

B. Students per computer in upper secondary education

Note: *Access among students to computers varies significantly across countries. More than 60 per cent of Danish households had a PC in 1998, compared with just 20 per cent of Italian households. And in Norway there were fewer than five students per computer in 1998, compared with as many as 35 per computer in Portugal.*

Source: OECD (2001g).

Key policy recommendations

If strategies to boost growth are to succeed, whether via ICT or any new technology, policies to enhance **human capital** (the skills and competencies embodied in labour) must be prioritised. Properly managed, many of these policies will also help to narrow the **digital and knowledge divides**:

- *Invest in high-quality early education and child care*: These investments are more cost-effective than later interventions to remedy school failure and they help boost participation in the labour market.

- *Raise completion of basic and vocational education and improve the quality of the system*: Dropout rates from secondary education have to be lowered. ICT literacy has become part of basic competencies and has to be improved, notably by recruiting qualified teachers and making pay more competitive.

- *Improve school-to-work transition*: Create or strengthen pathways that combine education with workplace experience; to ensure cost-effectiveness of the system, establish mechanisms of co-financing between employers, trainees and government.

- *Strengthen the links between higher education and the labour market in a cost-effective way*: This can be achieved through developing shorter course cycles with a healthy orientation to job market requirements. Involving firms in the definition of curricula and funding can be valuable, as can strengthening performance-based financial incentives.

- *Provide wider training opportunities*: Increase possibilities for adults and workers to participate in higher education. Innovative instruments, like individual learning accounts and systems of recognition of competencies, can enhance incentives to engage in training while helping to control costs. Ensure that firm training is not penalised by tax systems.

- *Reduce obstacles to workplace changes and give workers a greater voice*: Employee involvement and effective labour-management relationships and practices are key to foster change and raise productivity – governments must allow this to develop. Ensure that working time legislation and employment regulations do not hamper efficient organisational change; adapt collective bargaining institutions to the new economic environment.

Notes

1. Based on a new database, Bassanini and Scarpetta (2001) provide empirical support for the growth-enhancing role of human capital in OECD countries. Accordingly, one additional year of schooling would, on average, lead to about 6 per cent higher GDP in the long run. In Greece, Ireland, Italy and Spain, the improvement in human capital has accounted for over half a percentage point higher growth in the 1990s compared with the 1980s. These results contrast with earlier studies where an insignificant effect of education on growth was found. But, as de la Fuente and Domenech (2000) have shown, these earlier studies used a less comprehensive database.

2. This evaluation is based on a comparison of the school and labour market performance of individuals of age 27 who had participated in the early education programme, compared with non-participants of the same age (Schweinhart, 1993).

Chapter V.

Fostering Firm Creation and Entrepreneurship

V.I. Entrepreneurship varies across countries

Every period of technological change is a period of opportunity. Indeed, risk-taking and entrepreneurial activity feed on change, but also drive it. The pace of business formation has increased dramatically in several countries over the past decade, thanks largely to ICT, but also other new technologies, such as biotechnology. Newly created firms have spurred innovation in many areas. They have been responsible for an increasing share of the growth in private R&D and patent activity in the United States and a number of other countries[1] (United States Council of Economic Advisors, 2001; Schreyer, 2000b). The jobs they have created have tended to be knowledge intensive and highly skilled. Their working organisations has tended to be more flexible too, in terms of training, internal job mobility and reward (Coutrot, 2000). Overall, there is evidence that the contribution of start-ups in the ICT sector to overall MFP growth has increased in recent years. Given the special role played by innovative start-ups in the 1990s, this part of the report concentrates on identifying policies that help foster new firm creation and development.

At the same time, business failure among start-ups has also been marked. Not all entrepreneurs succeed, but far from being a sign of economic weakness, this dynamism in firm turnover (i.e. entry and exit) reflects the ability of countries to expand the boundaries of economic activity, shift resources and adjust the structure of production to meet consumers' changing needs. Indeed, as was explained in Chapter I, this "creative destruction" has been a boon for productivity growth.

While new innovative firms are present in all OECD countries, the level of new firm creation has differed widely (Figure V.1). The scarce evidence that is available suggests that start-up activity has been much higher in North America than in Europe or in Japan (Reynolds et al., 2000). There is a wide range of reasons for this, covering financial support, regulatory and administrative environments, education and training,

Figure V.1. **The level of entrepreneurial activity differs across OECD countries**

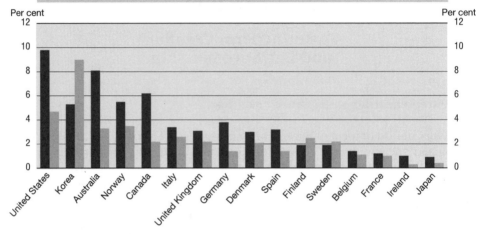

■ Start-up activity: Percentage of adults engaged in the process of creating a business in the past 12 months

■ New firm activity: Percentage of adults owning (solely or partly) and managing an operating business that is less than 42 months old

Note: The proportion of the adult population engaged in nascent and new firms varies significantly across countries. Survey results show that in the United States, one in every 10 adults was starting a business in 2000, compared with one in 100 in Japan. The number of adults engaged in new firms ranges from one in 11 in Korea to less than one in 200 in Japan.

Source: Reynolds et al. (2000).

and cultural and social issues (Figure V.2). Financial support, in particular the availability of risk-capital, is a problem in many countries. However, in countries where entrepreneurial activity is low, government regulations and cultural and social considerations also act as important constraints on entrepreneurship. The following sections discuss the contributions of these factors in more detail and the role of policy in enhancing their effectiveness.

V.2. Financing new innovative firms

The importance of venture capital

As just mentioned, one important impediment to entry for new innovative firms is the lack of financing. Start-ups obviously have no track record and, especially in

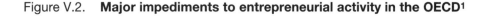

Figure V.2. **Major impediments to entrepreneurial activity in the OECD[1]**

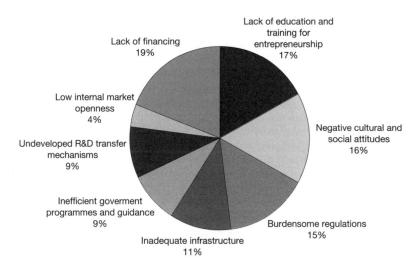

Note: *The pie chart illustrates the role of framework conditions for entrepreneurial activity in the OECD. Figures shown represent the frequency with which each issue was raised during interviews with entrepreneurs in 14 OECD countries. Access to financing represents an important problem for starting-up an enterprise, as do lack of education and training.*
1. Unweighted average of 14 OECD countries participating in the study.
Source: Reynolds *et al.* (2000).

the ICT sector, often very little collateral, which makes it difficult for them to obtain bank loans or other forms of debt financing. Personal savings and other informal sources (*e.g.* borrowing from friends and family) may help to raise some initial funds. But for the recent wave of innovative start-ups, the main source of funding has tended to be equity finance, whether venture capital or from so-called business angels. These private investors do more than just supply funds, they help start-ups to develop as businesses, providing advice and even management. They become crisis managers when times turn bad and contribute to firms' survival.

Innovative start-ups may not flourish in countries without a broad venture capital culture. And not all OECD countries have developed venture capital activity to the same extent. The United States invests more in this way as a percentage of GDP or per company than any other country, and informal private investment is believed to be greater than that again (Box V.1).

75|

Box V.1.   **Informal investors play an important role in the financing of start-ups**

Business angels are generally wealthy individuals with substantial business experience who invest directly in start-ups. They tend to focus more on early-stage financing than institutional investors and they provide more managerial and business advice through their greater personal involvement. Although data are scarce (partly because these individuals are hard to identify and are often reluctant to reveal exact information), total funding by business angels is estimated to be several times greater than all other forms of private equity finance. For example, the European Business Angels Network (EBAN) estimates the number of active investors in Europe at 125 000 and the number of potential investors at 1 million. The investment pools of available business angels finance is estimated at EUR 3 billion in the United Kingdom, 1.5 billion in the Netherlands, 300 million in Finland and 20 million in Ireland. Some countries, *e.g.* France, have introduced tax incentives to promote business angels investment.

Large companies are increasingly investing in entrepreneurial ventures in spin-offs or start-ups, especially in the United States. For instance, Microsoft acquired shares in 44 firms for USD 13 billion in 1999, and Intel in 35 firms for USD 5 billion . Much of the corporate interest is driven by the strategy of larger companies to diversify the sources of innovative activity. Through financing and co-operating with small innovative firms, larger firms can gain access to new technologies; small firms in return can benefit from the expertise of large corporations in fields such as marketing or services to customers. Corporate venture capital could reflect the changing relationship between large and small firms and the new dynamics of innovation.

New technology has clearly been the target of U.S. venture capitalists. Between 1995 and 1999, ICT, biotechnology and medical/health-related sectors absorbed more than 80 per cent of total venture capital investment. In contrast, in Japan and in the European Union, these high-tech industries attracted only about one quarter of venture capital investment[2] (Figure V.3). Moreover, in a number of European countries, in particular the United Kingdom, a large share of this investment was to finance acquisitions, rather than funding start-ups *per se*.

Regulations can inhibit the development of venture capital markets. One reason is the state of regulation on the type of investor eligible to supply venture capital funds. Rules in some countries still prevent or discourage pension funds, insurance companies and other institutions from venture capital investment. For example, pension funds are by far the most important source of venture capital

Figure V.3.   **Private venture capital investment by stage and sector**

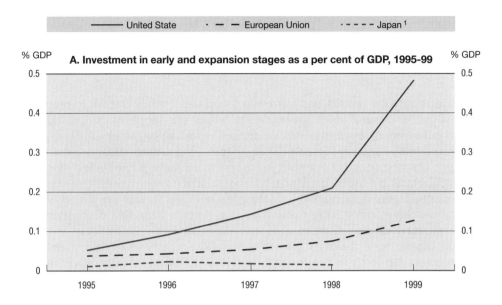

United State   · ▬ ▬ European Union   · - - - - Japan [1]

A. Investment in early and expansion stages as a per cent of GDP, 1995-99

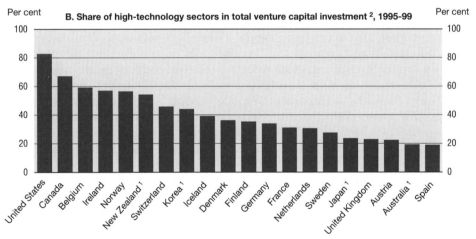

B. Share of high-technology sectors in total venture capital investment [2], 1995-99

Note: *Panel A shows that venture capital invested in early and expansion stages of firms is higher as a per cent of GDP and is growing much more rapidly in the United States than in the other two major OECD regions. Moreover, as shown in Panel B, a larger share of venture capital is invested in high-technology sectors in North America than elsewhere.*

1. Data refer to 1995-98.
2. Total venture capital investment includes early stage, expansion stage, buyouts and other.

Source: Baygan and Freudenberg (2000).

77|

in the United States, Australia and New Zealand, and play an important role in Finland, Sweden and the United Kingdom. In other European countries, like Germany, banks account for the majority of new funds raised by venture capital firms, while in some smaller countries (Norway, Ireland and Denmark) business angels dominate. In Japan and Korea, venture funds are raised mainly through corporations.

One reason for restrictions has been to protect certain classes of investors against over-exposure, which has tended to reduce the supply of risk-capital.[3] But as the gains from diversified portfolios, including technology stocks, may be great, several countries are now loosening their rules in a bid to channel more capital into this type of investment. For example, in Europe, four countries (the United Kingdom, Finland, Ireland and the Netherlands) have at present no legal restrictions – beyond general prudential requirement – on the type of investors that can invest in high capital-risk investment. Other countries, *e.g.* France, Italy, Spain, Sweden and Denmark, have taken actions to allow specific institutional investors to invest in venture capital. Nevertheless, removing quantitative constraints on risky investment still remains a priority in the majority of OECD countries. Clearly, governments have to find a balance between safeguarding against serious default or systemic fragility and the need to stimulate the supply of venture capital funding.

Taxation can also act as a barrier to the development of risk capital and tax reforms aimed at reducing distortions in this area should remain a priority in many countries. First, high tax rates on capital gains effectively imply double taxation of corporate retained earnings and therefore may negatively affect the supply of venture capital investment.[4] Such rates are relatively high in Japan, Canada and some EU countries. Second, tax rules generally tend to favour debt financing over new equity financing as corporate interest payments – as opposed to distributed profits – are usually deductible from corporate taxes. A few countries, *e.g.* Denmark, Finland and Italy, have recently introduced changes to their tax systems to ensure more equal treatment to the two forms of financing. Third, in some countries, especially in Europe, tax structures may also hinder cross-border investment by discriminating against foreign venture capital investors, for example through the double taxation of dividends in cross-border investment.

The role of high-risk capital markets

The degree of development of venture capital investment also goes hand-in-hand with the existence of well-functioning, accessible equity markets that facilitate the sale of assets, thus providing an exit mechanism that allows entrepreneurs and investors in early-stage risky projects to be compensated for their efforts. "New" markets, such as the NASDAQ in the United States or the Neuer Markt in Germany and the *nouveau marché* in France, play an important role in this regard. These markets typically have less stringent admission requirements and lower costs than the traditional main markets. Venture capital investors use them, through initial public offerings (IPOs), to pass along investments that have matured, re-liquefy their assets and seek new investment opportunities. An active IPO market is thus important to foster innovation by providing capital to new enterprises and raising additional funds for expanding firms. Market capitalisation has risen dramatically in these new equity markets during the past decade – notwithstanding the more recent decline[5] – but the level of initial public offerings remains much higher in the NASDAQ than elsewhere (Figure V.4). Some volatility is to be expected in technology equity markets given the risky nature of activities of companies listed on them. The fact remains that high-risk capital markets still have a critical role to play in financing innovation in the years to come.

Figure V.4. **"New" equity markets are developing in many OECD countries**[1]

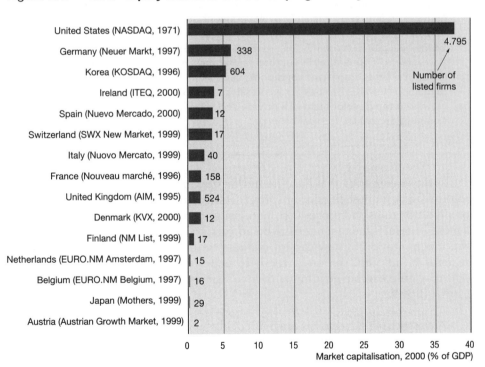

Note: *While "new" equity markets are developing in many OECD countries, market capitalisation as a per cent of GDP is still much higher in the US NASDAQ than elsewhere.*
1. Date in parentheses refers to the year in which the market was created.
Source: OECD (2001e).

Box V.2.   **Governments as venture capitalists in Europe**

In Europe, where venture capital markets are not yet sufficiently developed to enhance innovation, many governments have undertaken to supply venture capital directly or indirectly through participation in venture capital funds. Governments either aimed at the development of venture capital markets in general, or at meeting specific venture capital needs, such as limited funding for smaller undertakings. At the EU level, the European Commission and the European Investment Fund (EIF) sponsor a fund to encourage early stage investment in technology innovative companies. The Commission has also launched another special fund to support the creation of innovative small businesses. Other examples involve the EIF which in 1999 committed EUR 180 million to 31 funds located in 10 EU states, and the European Investment Bank which has the authority to use up to EUR 1 billion from its surpluses to back risk activities. Whether governments or public institutions should play this active role as venture capitalists is subject to debate. Public intervention may be warranted if it addresses identifiable market failures. Clearly, seed financing by government or public institutions may have a leveraging effect on private sector risk capital. But otherwise governments may not be the best placed to identify firms in which investment should take place. Moreover, government intervention in venture capital may be ineffective in boosting firm creation if other important conditions, such as management advice and proper regulations towards businesses, are missing. It may introduce distortions and even crowd out the development of a private sector venture capital market (European Commission, 2000a).

In those countries that have no new market, more effort should be made to reform stock market regulations, for instance by loosening overly restrictive qualification rules and procedures for registration and pricing methods. In Europe, a more general issue that needs to be addressed is that of consolidation. Indeed, the fragmentation of new capital markets, in part due to separate regulatory regimes in different countries, tends to impede the growth of venture capital. This may help explain governments' involvement in the direct supply of venture capital (Box V.2).

Such stock market reforms are particularly important to stimulate international venture capital flows. These can represent an important source of funding for start-ups. These flows are increasing rapidly. In fact, already in 1999 venture capital investments going to firms in Ireland and Denmark were almost four times larger than investments stemming from funds located in these countries (Figure V.5). As US investment enters a slower period, these global trends could sharpen as investors look more closely at opportunities elsewhere, *e.g.* in Europe and Asia.

Figure V.5. **Cross-border venture capital investment flows
in European countries**

Net inflows as a percentage of domestic investments, 1999

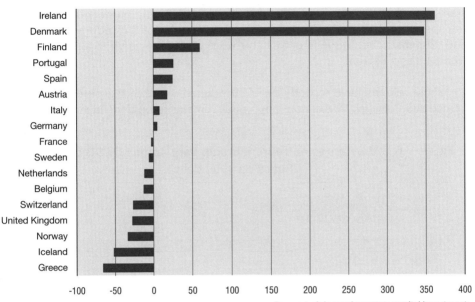

Per cent of domestic venture capital investment

Note: The graph compares net inflows of venture capital investment (i.e. inflows minus outflows) among
European countries with domestic investment. Ireland and Denmark are by far the largest recipients of
venture capital from abroad.

Source: Baygan and Freudenberg (2000).

Moreover, these start-ups could do better than some of those that featured in the
past few years, as their access to experienced venture capitalists should reduce
imprudent decision-making and expectations. International investors are becoming
more selective, so that countries that offer the best overall conditions for successful
innovation and the highest prospects for growth should attract the largest amount
of foreign high-risk capital.

V.3. Facilitating entrepreneurial activity

Amending administrative and bankruptcy regulations

High administrative barriers to start-ups are key in this respect. In a number of
countries, regulations in the registration of new businesses are either excessive or

81

© OECD 2001

unnecessarily complicated and drawn-out.[6] This obviously adds to the cost of firm creation and discourages entry. In 1998, formalities for establishing a company were relatively few in the United States, the United Kingdom and Denmark, but were many in France, Italy and Spain (Figure V.6). But it does not stop there; firms in their start-up and gestation phases may be disproportionately burdened by the non-transparency of tax and other administrative compliance procedures. Regulatory and administrative burdens of this sort were particularly high in Japan, Sweden, Denmark and Belgium.

Some reforms have recently been introduced or are in the pipeline (in Italy, France and Portugal, for example), but much remains to be done in many countries

Figure V.6. **Barriers to entrepreneurship vary across OECD countries** [1]
Based on 1998 data

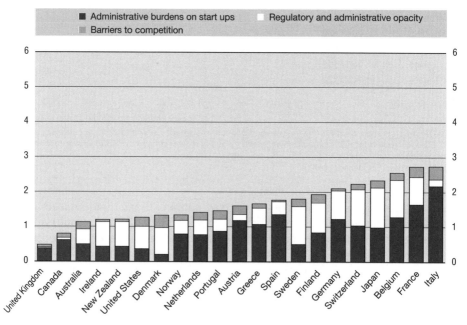

Note: In most OECD countries for which data are available, administrative barriers are the biggest single barrier to setting up new businesses. Barriers to competition, which include price controls and antitrust exemptions played less of a role in all countries.

1. The scale of indicators is 0-6, from least to most restrictive. Based on the situation in or around 1998. The components are weighted to show their relative importance in the overall indicator. Since 1998, many countries have implemented reforms. For some individual countries, more information on recent progress in regulatory reform (including an update of the indicators) can be found in the OECD Reviews of Regulatory Reform.

Source: Nicoletti et al. (1999).

to improve matters for new businesses. Initiatives taken in some countries to bring all administrative formalities together under one roof, providing clients with a "one-stop shop" and more centralised procedures represent steps in the right direction.[7] Governments could also promote on-line registrations and filing to reduce establishment and tax compliance costs. In addition, they could improve matters in the field of information and communication through the wider use of Internet portals. Overall, reducing burdensome administrative regulations is likely to contribute to faster MFP growth (Figure V.7).

Figure V.7. **There is a link between changes in multi-factor productivity (MFP) growth and administrative barriers to start-ups**

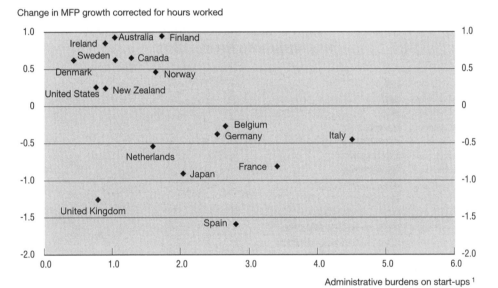

Change in MFP growth corrected for hours worked

Administrative burdens on start-ups[1]

Note: *Countries with the lowest administrative barriers to entrepreneurship have also registered the largest increase in MFP growth over the 1990s. Correlation coefficient: -0.51; T statistic: -2.32.*

1. The scale of indicators is 0-6, from least to most restrictive. Based on the situation in or around 1998. Since 1998, many countries have implemented reforms. For some individual countries, more recent regulatory information (including an update of the indicators), can be found in the OECD Reviews of Regulatory Reform.

Source: Nicoletti *et al.* (1999); MFP from Figure I.5.

Would-be entrepreneurs can be put off not just by barriers to entry, but by costs and difficulties to exiting business as well. High bankruptcy and insolvency costs, in particular, are a problem in several countries. Moreover, an overly stringent bankruptcy policy, while perhaps conducive to prudent decision-making among managers, may limit incentives to undertake risky projects with possible high future returns, leading to less innovation and, indeed, slower growth in the long run.

83

Bankruptcy provisions are less stringent in Canada and the United States than elsewhere. Indeed, an individual can declare bankruptcy, settle outstanding debts as far as possible from existing assets and start over another business shortly thereafter (Figure V.8). In most European countries, discharge from bankruptcy takes much longer; sometimes people who go bankrupt are required to settle their debt in full, which virtually prevents them from engaging again in future business. Other provisions of European countries' bankruptcy laws, such as restrictions on acting as a company director and on the provision of capital by banks, *de facto* eliminate the possibility of a second chance. Reviewing overly stringent bankruptcy and insolvency legislation should become a priority in most European countries, though the interests of creditors

Figure V.8. **Length of time that creditors have claims on a bankrupt's assets, 2000**

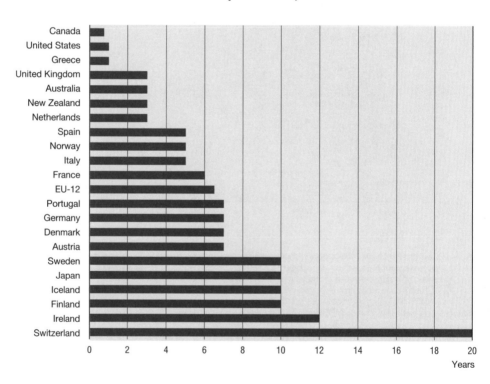

Note: In Canada and the United States, the discharge period after bankruptcy is one year or less. In comparison, in Switzerland creditors can retain their claims on bankrupt assets up to 20 years.

Source: OECD (2001e).

should obviously be kept in mind. In Japan and Korea, the absence of automatic creditor protection provides little incentives to declare bankruptcy, allowing crippled companies to continue their operations. This low rate of exit of unsuccessful companies is an important impediment to these economies' restructuring process and may limit productivity growth. It also restricts entrepreneurial activity. There is therefore an urgent need to review bankruptcy laws in these countries as part of the broader corporate sector reform.

Facilitating the use of employee ownership schemes

Employee ownership schemes, such as broad-based stock options plans[8] can help ease the entry of new firms. Indeed, they represent an attractive way for firms to compensate employees as they are not treated as conventional employment costs and therefore do not affect profit and loss performance. In addition, employee ownership schemes serve to attract, motivate and retain employees, particularly in the early stages of development when the viability of start-ups is uncertain. There are also indications that broad-based stock options, along with other employee share schemes, raise performance and enhance productivity through better alignment of employees' and management's interests (Black and Lynch, 2000; Lebow et al., 1999).

The use of stock options varies widely across OECD countries. The tax treatment they are accorded is one of the reasons for this. The taxation of stock options raises many complex issues such as the classification of income – i.e. compensation versus investment income – and the risk of excessive and double taxation. A number of countries, including France, Germany, Japan, the Netherlands, the United Kingdom and the United States, have already changed their tax provisions to address some of these issues. As a general principle, countries should ensure that their tax system is neutral vis-à-vis this form of compensation, so that it does not discourage start-ups from taking advantage of it.

Making government programmes more efficient

Governments have put in place a myriad of schemes to assist start-ups in recent years. These schemes, designed in principle to overcome market failures have at times led to the subsidisation of non-viable firms and impeded exit. As a general rule, governments should assess the relevance and effectiveness of their support programmes towards small enterprises with a view to streamlining or terminating those whose rationale and efficiency is questionable.

Local authorities can play a useful indirect role in encouraging private initiatives at the local level in partnership with local players. While proper evaluation of cost-effectiveness remains essential, these authorities can for example contribute to the development of incubators, which help provide infrastructure, on-site advice on the availability of skilled labour and training opportunities as well as information on venture capital suppliers. Similarly, they can lock-in some of the benefits of existing geographical clusters that have spawned naturally – Silicon Valley is but one celebrated example, there are probably thousands of others located across the OECD area – by promoting the establishment of inter-firm networks, such as suppliers' associations, and assuring effective public services.

V.4. The role of education and training and social attitudes

Better policies are a necessary but insufficient condition of entrepreneurship. Opportunities also need a sufficient pool of entrepreneurs. Surveys conducted in a number of countries show that only a limited share of the working-age population between 25 and 44 is engaged in firm start-up activity. Moreover, there are more men entrepreneurs than women, although countries with the highest level of entrepreneurial activity are also those where women are most engaged. In particular, there is evidence that over the past five years, women entrepreneurs have increasingly taken advantage of new business opportunities created by ICT to start up firms, especially in Canada and the United States. Nevertheless, much remains to be done in many countries to promote a pro-entrepreneurial culture. This however is a complex matter which to a large depends extent on how entrepreneurs are perceived in society at large.

In addition to policies discussed in Chapter IV, education and training systems have a key role to play in creating positive attitudes towards entrepreneurship and in providing adequate managerial skills targeted at start-ups. Levels of entrepreneurial activity are more depressed in countries where educational systems do not offer adequate programmes for training potential and practising entrepreneurs. Survey results indicate that entrepreneurship is low in countries where there are major shortages of the skills needed to convert business opportunities into market realities (Reynolds *et al.*, 2000).

Graduate students enrolled in MBA programmes make up a significant proportion of the people that might potentially get involved in entrepreneurial activity and there is in fact a positive link between MBA enrolment and entrepreneurship (European Commission, 2000*b*). Secondary and tertiary schools and colleges could be encouraged to make more of an effort to offer courses and programmes on entrepreneurship to wider cohorts, not just MBA students. Programmes bringing together training providers, universities, business schools, as well as firms and private investors, could also be designed to identify best practices and propose changes to existing curricula. Finally, as stressed in Chapter III, policies should encourage researchers to become more entrepreneurial too.

Key policy recommendations

Entrepreneurship has always been important, but its role stands out in the present time of innovative change. Fostering a climate to help instil greater dynamism in the creation and expansion of firms is fundamental.

- *Promote access to financing*: Reform those regulations and fiscal provisions that inhibit the development of venture and high-risk capital markets and limit the supply of capital for risky and innovative undertakings.

- *Facilitate firm entry and exit*: Eliminate burdensome administrative regulations and those features of tax systems that afflict particularly smaller, technologically driven, young firms; review overly stringent bankruptcy and insolvency provisions where they eliminate the possibility for entrepreneurs to have a second chance; ensure that tax systems are neutral towards the use of innovative employee ownership/remuneration schemes.

- *Review and assess the relevance and effectiveness of government support programmes*: Adapt policy orientations and programmes that risk becoming obsolete more quickly than before, hampering firm growth or slowing the exit of non-competitive firms; identify and encourage best practices in government programmes, *e.g.* "one-stop shops" for administrative formalities.

- *Encourage an entrepreneurial spirit in society*: Instil a positive attitude towards entrepreneurship, through education and provision of managerial training.

Notes

1. This trend may also reflect strategies of larger companies towards the diversification of their R&D activities. They can do so either by transferring their research activities into a new entity which they finance directly, or by investing in innovative start-ups. In this case, the experience shows that large corporations tend to take them over when they succeed (see Box V.1).

2. This share varies widely across different countries in Europe, however.

3. The US experience suggests that the removal of quantitative constraints following the 1978 decision to relax the "Prudent Man Regulation" concerning institutional investment in risk capital provided a major impetus to this type of capital.

4. This happened in the United States, where high-risk capital investment accelerated in the early 1980s, following the 1978 reduction in capital gains, and decelerated after the 1986 Tax Reform Act which included an increase in capital gain taxation.

5. Since March 2000, capitalisation in many European and US new markets has registered large falls. This has raised concerns about the long-term ability of new equity markets to allocate funds and promote innovative businesses. The downturn in the new markets is probably a correction from previously overvalued prices and optimism about returns. While investors are certainly exercising greater prudence now, being more selective about their investments, whether new markets will stabilise or rise again sharply remains an open question.

6. Administrative barriers and regulatory costs may also affect the growth of existing business, in particular for smaller firms (OECD, 2001j).

7. The length of time to establish a company has been substantially reduced – from several weeks to a few days – in countries such as France, Ireland, Denmark and Portugal, for example.

8. In the 1990s, stock options were a standard feature in most executive pay packages in the United States and their use expanded in other OECD countries. More recently, the use of stock options has been extended to a larger population of workers in firms. Broad-based stock options allow those who accept the risk associated with working for dynamic, but unproven, start-ups to share their potential success.

Chapter VI.

Getting the Fundamentals Right

Policies on ICT, human capital, innovation and firm creation rely on fundamental economic and social stability to succeed. All of the policy areas discussed in the previous chapters are interlinked and depend on each other for new growth opportunities to be realised. But those countries that have managed to lift their growth potential were able to do so because they had been getting their fundamentals right. They owed their economic success to sound macroeconomic policies, well-functioning institutions and markets, and an orientation to build a more open and competitive economic environment (Box VI.1). By contrast, in those countries whose growth performances appeared to lag, some of the fundamentals were perhaps missing or were at best so weak as to make it difficult to harness the new dynamism, such as not having the right institutional set-up for new business creation.

Box VI.1.   **Changes in policy frameworks in successful countries**

Those OECD countries whose GDP per capita stood markedly higher in the last decade than in the 1980s owe a good deal of their economic success to changes in macroeconomic and structural policies, some of which were initiated in the 1980s or earlier. In most of them, the improvement in the cyclically-adjusted budget balance has been sharp, turning often large structural deficits into large structural surpluses. Public sector reforms carried out in Australia, Finland and Sweden have enhanced the efficiency and transparency of public spending and administration as well. Tax reforms in Ireland and Australia have improved these countries' overall investment environments. In the majority, inflation has been kept under control, thanks to a combination of sound monetary policy and wage moderation, like in the Netherlands and Finland, or radical changes in the monetary policy frameworks, as was the case in Canada and Sweden.

Box VI.1. **Changes in policy frameworks in successful countries** (*cont.*)

Structural and regulatory reforms have been an integral part of the improvements witnessed in these countries – even if the structural agenda is still unfinished – and have no doubt interacted positively with appropriate macroeconomic policies. In the United States and Finland, for example, early and far-reaching liberalisation of the telecommunications sector boosted competition in dynamic segments of the ICT market. External forces, such as joining the European Single Market for Ireland and Sweden, or greater exposure to competition from international producers for the United States, Canada and Australia, have also played a role in making these countries more adaptable to change. Financial market liberalisation has been a key ingredient too. A deep and liquid financial market has been essential in funding new innovative activities in the United States. And changes that took place in the wake of the banking crises in Sweden and Finland made this sector more competitive and open to the speedy adoption of new technologies. Labour market reforms have also figured prominently in Canada, Australia, Ireland, the Netherlands and Finland. Education and training systems have also undergone profound changes, underpinning a rapid improvement in skill levels, greater competence in applying ICT and more openness to technological and organisational change.

VI.1. Sound macroeconomic policies

Stable macroeconomic policies have a critical role to play in enabling economic changes that are conducive to higher growth of GDP per capita and MFP. Fiscal discipline, low inflation rates and the reduction in the variability of inflation over the 1990s have helped to boost national savings, reducing uncertainty and enhancing the efficiency of the price mechanisms in allocating resources.[1] This has resulted in an improved environment for decision making and has unleashed resources for private investment. Clearly, these sound policies work and have to be maintained.

At the same time, the way public finances are improved influences growth. In particular, government is a direct investor in the economy. Although the volume of this investment may be small compared with that of the private sector, it can have a telling effect. For example, public investment in R&D, transport, communication and infrastructure, to the extent it is of high quality and generates high economic and social returns, can help to create an environment conducive to entrepreneurship, innovation and private sector activity. Similarly, efficient government spending on education should improve the stock of human capital (see Chapter IV). Less than a fifth of public expenditure is however typically allocated to these growth-enhancing areas in OECD countries. Exceptions are Norway, Denmark, Portugal, Australia and

Sweden which stand out for their higher-than-average share in this respect. The pursuit of fiscal consolidation should of course remain a priority, particularly in view of population ageing, but neglecting public spending in high-return physical and human capital investments can lead to negative economic effects in the medium- term. Budgets may have to be readjusted accordingly.

Government consumption and social transfers can also have some impact on growth, whether or not this is their main purpose. It is sometimes argued that social transfers may even have a direct impact through their effect on income distribution. The evidence on this is far from clear-cut though (Box VI.2). In all cases, expenditures

---

Box VI.2. **Is income inequality good or bad for growth?**

There are two clear-cut views on this question. According to one view, income inequality can be good for growth. The main plank of this argument is that a large income differential provides an incentive to invest in human capital and save. The larger the differential, the stronger the incentive for acquiring the kind of competencies that lead to high-wage jobs. In contrast, a compressed distribution of income could indicate a small reward for investing and saving, thereby inhibiting growth.

But inequality may also be bad for growth. Though the prospect of earning more provides low-income individuals with an incentive to invest, low-income individuals may not be able to access the capital they need to make the necessary investments. In education and training for instance, there is no physical asset which can be reclaimed by a bank in the event of a non-performing loan. The result is that an uneven income distribution could be associated with lower investment in human capital than is the case when income is more evenly distributed. Moreover, an uneven distribution of income may erode political support for policies to enhance growth if people do not see any direct gain for them. For example, while there may be large net gains from opening an economy to trade, those who have been working in activities which become not viable because of foreign competition, in particular the low-skilled, could lose their current jobs from such a policy. These groups may have a strong incentive to block such liberalising policies.

A recent OECD study shows that there is no robust evidence in support of either view (OECD, 2001k). Certainly, the recent cross-country growth performance of OECD countries cannot be explained by differences in income distribution. This does not mean that income inequality is neither good nor bad for growth, but that the possible growth impacts of inequality are probably small compared with some of the other factors discussed in this report. Moreover, a wide income inequality may be an issue of policy concern in and of itself, whatever its links to growth.

91

have to be financed. Where taxes are raised to support government spending, tax pressure can become excessive and undermine growth. In fact, rising tax pressures may have negatively affected growth in GDP per capita in countries such as Finland, Norway, Portugal and Spain over the 1990s (OECD, 2000f).

VI.2. Encouraging openness

One of the main drivers behind promoting technological innovation and productivity gains has been the expansion of markets world-wide. Progress in reducing tariff barriers, dismantling non-tariff barriers and liberalising capital markets has opened up opportunities in trade and international investment.[2] The United States and Canada, but also small open economies like Australia, Ireland and Spain have taken the largest advantage of this trend (Bassanini et al. 2001). The reasons are simple: openness increases the size of markets available to innovators and consumers, while facilitating the spread of knowledge, technologies and new business practices.

Maintaining an open policy stance remains essential. It will contribute to cut costs through further tariff liberalisation of trade in ICT related products. It will also encourage the adoption of international standards which everyone can agree to and which protect consumers and innovators alike. Indeed, well-designed trade policies can accelerate the development of electronic commerce, for instance, by removing some of the uncertainty that hangs over it today. In other words, continued progress in opening markets to international trade and capital is essential for growth, while keeping in mind the constant needs to adapt the rules and practices to the changing global landscape.

Openness is not just about markets of course. It is also about culture and a readiness for change. All of the countries where MFP growth has risen appear to share these features. Indeed, this is arguably the feature that characterises the current period of change most: not just the importance of ideas and knowledge to economic growth but, as seen in Chapters III and IV, what matters too is that these be transferred and shared among economic agents. As already discussed in previous parts of this report, governments can help to enhance this atmosphere of creative openness.

VI.3. Efficient financial and product markets

Financial systems have to be supportive of innovation

As seen in Chapters III and V, methods of financing have evolved in many countries to foster and accompany the development and diffusion of innovation and ICT and address the specific needs of start-ups and of R&D. Financial institutions in many countries have to adapt so that they are not solely geared towards the accumulation of physical assets in large, stable firms and well-established industries, but also geared up to supply funds for investment in more risky, innovative, undertakings.

The relationship between growth of new innovative firms and financial systems across countries requires policies that ensure that contracts are enforced and that accurate information on performance is disseminated in a timely manner. Such policies on balance spur innovative activities (Leahy *et al.*, 2001). Of course, one problem with new firms and innovative investment is the difficulty of assessing prospects. This is why sound management principles and transparency are such an important form of protection for investors. Any reforms to domestic financial markets should aim to create that mix of transparency and protection that innovative risk-taking requires.

Competitive product markets

Recent growth in new areas of business has owed much to competition and reform in product markets, such as telecommunications. Better product market regulation and a more competitive environment have sped up the adoption of new technologies and, more generally, the process of innovation and growth. Broad initiatives, like the completion of the Single Market in Europe, have contributed to market openness. However, state controls over prices and market entry for instance, still interfere widely with competition and productivity growth. Yet there is a widespread consensus among governments of the importance of competition for dynamic changes to take hold. Transposing that belief into action remains a challenge in several countries.

VI.4. Well-functioning labour markets and social protection

Well-functioning labour markets are essential in periods of technological change. To minimise the potential hardship that change can create, labour market institutions have to ensure that affected workers are given the support and the incentives they need to find new jobs and possibly to retrain. This has been emphasised in the OECD Jobs Study and institutions and regulations that hinder the mobility of workers and prevent the rapid and efficient reallocation of labour resources must be reviewed in many countries.

The benefits of growth should be shared among the entire population. One of the best ways to achieve this is to boost participation in the labour market. A number of countries have done this (OECD, 2000j). However, more has to be done. More effective active labour market programmes, such as counselling schemes, training programmes,

93

wage subsidies and targeted measures on disadvantaged groups, if well designed, can contribute to attract people in the labour market, prevent long-term unemployment and increase the productivity of workers who participate in the programmes. This may also be good for growth; the evidence shows that the increase in active social spending in 1984-97 in the OECD area may have led to a rise in GDP of nearly 1 per cent (OECD, 2001*k*).[3] Likewise, making-work pay policies, such as the US earned income tax credit, the working families tax credit in the United Kingdom and the family income supplement in Ireland, can encourage labour market participation of would-be workers. Such employment-oriented social policies would contribute to achieving higher levels of labour utilisation in countries where they are currently low. As pointed out in Chapter I, this represents an important factor for stimulating faster growth in GDP per capita.

In short, well-designed social protection would not only tackle inequalities but also contribute to growth. It will also increase support for the other policies advocated in this report which promote rapid economic restructuring.

Key policy recommendations

Ensuring that the economic and social **fundamentals** are in place is an essential part of any comprehensive growth strategy:

- *Preserve macroeconomic stability*: Maintain or enhance fiscal discipline and keep inflation low to reduce uncertainty, increase economic efficiency and free up resources for high-return private investment.

- *Encourage openness*: Reduce barriers to competition and maintain an open policy stance for international trade and investment so as to reduce costs, improve international standards and promote e-commerce. Openness is fundamental to promote the diffusion of ideas and knowledge world-wide.

- *Make financial systems more supportive of innovation*: Implement reforms to create a mix of greater firm transparency and investor protection to foster innovative investment and enterprise.

- *Mobilise labour resources*: Reform institutions so that new jobs opportunities arise throughout the economy; encourage mobility and help workers affected by change.

- *Address the redistributive implications of structural change*: Make labour market programmes and social policies more effective in bringing would-be workers into the job market. Ensure that the benefits of growth are shared by all.

Notes

1. Strong empirical support for these findings is presented by Bassanini *et al.* (2001).

2. Trade and investment policies have played an important role in helping OECD economies respond to technology-driven changes. Important steps were taken during the Uruguay Round, notably in the fields of intellectual property protection, liberalisation in services, and technical barriers to trade. Since, action has been taken to adapt the trading system to electronic business; *e.g.* through the 1996 Information Technology Agreement, the 1997 Agreement on Basic Telecommunications Services, and the 1998 Declaration on Global Electronic Commerce. Efforts are currently underway to address barriers to trade in ICT products and to liberalise ICT-using services further.

3. This estimate already accounts for the growth-depressing effect of higher taxes needed to finance active social spending.

Conclusions

Governments today are faced with a new economic environment. ICT has emerged as a key technology with the potential to transform economic and social activity and has led to more rapid growth in countries where the conditions for macroeconomic stability are in place. While it is too early to say how important ICT's transformations will be compared with those of previous innovations, like electricity, governments should nonetheless take action to manage adjustment and keep the social costs low. All governments can do more to exploit this new technology further, by accelerating its diffusion, providing the right skills and building confidence.

But ICT is not the only factor explaining growth disparities and policies to bolster these technologies will not on their own steer countries on to a higher growth path. Indeed, growth is not the result of a single policy or institutional arrangement, but a comprehensive and co-ordinated set of actions to create the right conditions for future change and innovation. This depends more than ever on improving the quality of human capital and responding to the changing demands of the workplace and society more broadly. It also means providing more scope for risk-takers to explore the new business opportunities that come with economic change. At the same time, the importance of fundamentals has not lessened. If anything, the pivotal role of sound macroeconomic management has been underlined. Moreover, the significance of openness to trade, investment and ideas, as well as well-functioning economic and social institutions has been reaffirmed.

The key policy requirements arising from this report are summarised below and are shown in more detail at the end of each chapter. Policymakers have to be prepared to invest time and political capital in meeting these challenges. Many of the countries that achieved higher growth rates in the 1990s reaped the fruits of their earlier efforts, notably their macroeconomic and structural policy changes of the 1980s. In other words, while innovation may be rapid, it can take several years to create the kind of dynamic environment in which it might take place, let alone see the results.

Policy action will also require further examination of a range of thorny, yet unanswered issues. There is a major knowledge gap regarding which impact, if any, the new economic environment will have on the shape and duration of the business cycle. A close watch of the current slowdown in the United States and the behaviour of productivity over the next year or two will be valuable for gathering evidence about this. Looking ahead, growth prospects will also depend on the extent to which other innovations, such as biotechnology, influence economic systems, while the role of human and social capital in growth will require further investigation. Other changes will also have a role to play, such as the ageing of OECD populations and international migration. A better understanding of society's ability to deal with these changes will therefore be essential.

Key policy recommendations

While specific policy priorities may differ across countries, this report encourages governments to adopt a comprehensive growth strategy based on a combination of actions in order to:

1. **Strengthen economic and social fundamentals**, by ensuring macroeconomic stability, encouraging openness, improving the functioning of markets and institutions, and addressing the distributive consequences of change.

2. **Facilitate the diffusion of ICT**, by increasing competition in telecommunications and technology, improving skills, building confidence and making electronic government a priority.

3. **Foster innovation**, by giving greater priority to fundamental research, improving the effectiveness of public R&D funding, and promoting the flow of knowledge between science and industry.

4. **Invest in human capital**, by strengthening education and training, making the teaching profession more attractive, improving the links between education and the labour market and adapting labour market institutions to the changing nature of work.

5. **Stimulate firm creation**, by improving access to high-risk finance, reducing burdensome administrative regulations and instilling positive attitudes towards entrepreneurship.

References

BASSANINI, A., S. SCARPETTA and I. VISCO (2000),
"Knowledge, technology and economic growth: recent evidence from OECD countries", OECD *Economics Department Working Paper* No. 259, Paris.

BASSANINI, A. and S. SCARPETTA (2001),
"Does human capital matter for growth in OECD Countries? Evidence from pooled mean-group estimates", OECD *Economics Department Working Paper* No. 289, Paris.

BASSANINI, A., S. SCARPETTA and P. HEMMINGS (2001),
"Economic Growth: The Role of Policies and Institutions. Panel Data Evidence from OECD Countries", OECD *Economics Department Working Paper* No. 283, Paris.

BAYGAN, G. and M. FREUDENBERG (2000),
"The internationalisation of venture capital activity in OECD countries: Implications for measurement and policy", STI *Working Paper* 2000/7, Paris.

BLACK, S.E. and L.M. LYNCH (2000),
"What's driving the new economy: the benefits of workplace innovation", NBER *Working Paper Series* 7479, Cambridge, MA.

BRANSCOMB, L.M. (1999),
"The false dichotomy: scientific creativity and utility", *Issues in Science and Technology*, Fall 1999.

COLECCHIA, A. (2001),
"The impact of Information Communications Technology on output growth", STI *Working Paper*, OECD, Paris, forthcoming.

COMMISSION OF THE EUROPEAN COMMUNITIES (2000a),
"Benchmarking enterprise policy – First results from the scoreboard", Commission Staff Working Document SEC(2000) 1841, Brussels.

COMMISSION OF THE EUROPEAN COMMUNITIES (2000b),
"Progress report on the risk capital action plan", *European Economy, Supplement* A, No. 8/9, August-September, Brussels.

COUTROT, T. (2000),
Innovations et gestion de l'emploi, Dares, 2000.03, No. 12.1, ministère de l'Emploi et de la Solidarité, Paris.

DE LA FUENTE, A. and R. DOMENECH (2000),
"Human capital in growth regressions, how much difference does data quality make?", CSIC, Campus de la Universidad Autonome de Barcelona.

GORDON, R.J. (2000),
"Does the 'New Economy' Measure up to the Great Inventions of the Past?", NBER Working Paper, No.7833, NBER, Cambridge, MA, August.

GUELLEC, D. and B. VAN POTTELSBERGHE DE LA POTTERIE (2000),
"The Impact of public R&D expenditure on business R&D", STI Working Paper 2000/4, OECD, Paris.

GUELLEC, D. and B. VAN POTTELSBERGHE DE LA POTTERIE (2001),
"R&D and productivity growth: A panel analysis of 16 OECD countries", STI Working Paper 2001/3, OECD, Paris.

GUISO, L., P. SAPIENZA and L. ZINGALES (2000),
"The role of social capital in financial development", NBER Working Paper, No. 7563, February.

JAFFE, A.B. (1999),
"The US patent system in transition: Policy innovation and the innovation process", NBER Working Paper, No. 7280, NBER, Cambridge, MA.

LEAHY, M., S. SCHICH, G. WEHINGER, F. PELGRIN and T. THORGEIRSSON (2001),
"Contributions for Financial Systems to Growth in OECD Countries", OECD Economics Department Working Papers No. 280, OECD, Paris.

LEBOW, D., L. SHEINER, L. SLIFMAN, M. STARR-McCLUER (1999),
"Recent Trends in Compensation Practices", Board of Governors of the Federal Reserve System, Washington, D.C., mimeo.

LITAN, R.E. and A.M. RIVLIN (2000),
"The economy and the Internet: What lies ahead?", Conference Report No. 4, Brookings Institution, Washington, D.C., December.

MADDISON, A. (1995),
Monitoring the world economy 1820-1992, Development Centre Studies, OECD, Paris.

MCMILLAN, G.S., F. NARIN and D.L. DEEDS (2000),
"An analysis of the critical role of public science in innovation: the case of biotechnology", Research Policy, Vol. 29, pp. 1-8.

MOWERY, D.C. and A.A. ZIEDONIS (2000),

"Numbers, quality and entry: How has the Bayh-Dole Act affected US University patenting and licensing?", in: A. JAFFE, J. LERNER and S. STERN, *Innovation Policy and the Economy*, MIT Press, forthcoming.

NICOLETTI, G., S. SCARPETTA and O. BOYLAUD (1999),

"Summary indicators of product market regulation with an extension to employment protection legislation", OECD *Economics Department Working Paper No.* 226, Paris.

NORDHAUS, W.D. (2001*b*),

"Productivity Growth and the New Economy", NBER *Working Paper*, No. 8096, Cambridge, MA.

OECD (1995),

Purchasing Power Parities and Real Expenditures, Vol. 1, 1993, Paris.

OECD (1999*a*),

Employment Outlook, Paris.

OECD (2000*a*),

Measuring the ICT *sector*, Paris.

OECD (2000*b*),

OECD *Economic Survey of Finland* (2000), Paris.

OECD (2000*c*),

"Recent growth trends in OECD countries", OECD *Economic Outlook*, No. 67, Paris.

OECD (2000*d*),

Purchasing Power Parities and Real Expenditures, 1996 *Results*, Paris.

OECD (2000*e*),

"Local Access Pricing and E-commerce", DSTI/ICCP/TISP(2000)1/FINAL, Paris, *http://www.oecd.org/dsti/sti/it/cm/prod/localaccess.htm*

OECD (2000*f*),

"Links between policy and growth: cross-country evidence", OECD *Economic Outlook*, No. 68, Paris, pp. 133-154.

OECD (2000*g*),

A *New Economy? The Changing Role of Innovation and Information Technology in Growth*, Paris.

OECD (2000*h*),

Science, Technology and Industry Outlook 2000, Paris.

OECD (2000i),

Where are the Resources for Lifelong Learning?, Paris.

OECD (2000j),
Employment Outlook, Paris.

OECD (2001a),
"Productivity and firm dynamics: Evidence from Microdata", OECD Economic Outlook, No. 69, Paris.

OECD (2001b),
Impacts of Electronic Commerce on Business, Paris, forthcoming.

OECD (2001c),
OECD Communications Outlook 2001, Paris.

OECD (2001d),
Competition Issues in Electronic Commerce, DAFFE/CLP (2000) 32, Paris, January, http://www.oecd.org/daf/clp/Roundtables/e-com.pdf

OECD (2001e),
Drivers of Growth: Information Technology, Innovation and Entrepreneurship, Paris, forthcoming.

OECD (2001f),
Knowledge, Work Organisation and Economic Growth, Paris.

OECD (2001g),
Education Policy Analysis, Paris.

OECD (2001h),
Thematic Review of Early Childhood Education and Care Policy, Paris.

OECD (2001i),
The Well-being of Nations: The Role of Human and Social Capital, Paris.

OECD (2001j),
Business Views' on Red Tape. A Survey of Administrative and Regulatory Environments of Small and Medium-sized Enterprises, Paris, forthcoming.

OECD (2001k)
Growth, Inequality and Social Protection, Paris.

OULTON, N. (2001),
"ICT and Productivity Growth in the UK", Bank of England, January.

PILAT, D. and LEE, F. (2001),
"Productivity growth in ICT-producing and ICT-using industries: A source of growth differentials in the OECD?", STI Working Paper 2001/4, Paris.

REYNOLDS, P., M. HAY, W. BYGRAVE, S. CAMP and E. AUTIO (2000),
"Global entrepreneurship monitor – 2000 executive report", Kauffman Center for Entrepreneurial Leadership at the Ewing Marion Kauffman Foundation.

RYCROFT, R.W. and D.E. KASH (1999),
"Innovation policy for complex technologies", *Issues in Science and Technology*, Autumn.

SCARPETTA, S., A. BASSANINI, D. PILAT and P. SCHREYER (2000),
"Economic growth in the OECD area: Recent trends at the aggregate and sectoral levels", OECD *Economics Department Working Paper No. 248*, Paris.

SCHREYER, P. (2000*a*),
"The Contribution of information and communication technologies to output growth"; STI *Working Paper* 2000/2, OECD, Paris.

SCHREYER, P. (2000*b*),
"High-growth firms and employment", STI *Working Paper* 2000/3, OECD, Paris.

SCHREYER, P. (2001),
"Computer price indices and international growth and productivity comparisons", OECD Statistics Directorate, Paris, April.

SCHWEINHART, L.J. (1993),
Significant Benefits: The High/Scope Perry Preschool Study through age 27, Ypsilanti, MI, The High/Scope Press.

SOLOW, R.M. (1987),
"We'd better watch out", *New York Times*, July 12, Book Review, No. 36.

STIGLITZ, J.E. (1999),
"Knowledge in the modern economy", in: DEPARTMENT OF TRADE AND INDUSTRY, *Our Competitive Future – The Economics of the Knowledge Driven Economy*, pp. 37-57. London, December.

TRIPLETT, J.E. (1999),
"The Solow productivity paradox: What do computers do to productivity", *Canadian Journal of Economics*, Vol. 32, No. 2, pp. 309-334.

UNITED STATES COUNCIL OF ECONOMIC ADVISORS (2001),
Economic Report of the President, Washington.

VAN DER WIEL, H. (2000),
"ICT important for growth", CPB *Report* 2000/2, pp. 17-23, CPB Netherlands Bureau for Economic Policy Analysis, The Hague.

WHELAN, K. (2000),
"Computers, obsolescence and productivity", *Finance and Economics Discussion Series* 2000-20, Federal Reserve Board, Washington, D.C.

WILLMS, J.D. (2000),
"Three Hypotheses about Community Effects Relevant to the Contribution of Human and Social Capital to Sustaining Economic Growth and Well-Being", Paper presented at Symposium on the Contribution of Human and Social Capital to Sustained Economic Growth and Well-being, Quebec, 20-21 March.

OECD PUBLICATIONS, 2, rue André-Pascal, 75775 PARIS CEDEX 16
PRINTED IN FRANCE
(92 2001 09 1 P) ISBN 92-64-18729-4 – No.51979 2001